BRITISH FIGURATIVE ART

British Figurative Art

PART ONE: PAINTING
THE HUMAN FIGURE

Martin Gayford

momentum

British Figurative Art, Part 2: Sculpture
will be published in August 1998

First published in Great Britain in 1997 by
Momentum, P.O. Box 12752, London E8 3UA

ISBN 1 873362 64 1 (paper)
ISBN 1 873362 65 X (cased)

A catalogue record for this book is available from the British Library

Co-ordinated by Ben Lawrence and Kate Leese
Designed by Peter Gladwin

Printed in London by The Pale Green Press

Flowers East
199 – 205 Richmond Road
London E8 3NJ
Telephone 0181-985 3333
Facsimile 0181-985 0067

When the poet Samuel Rogers returned from Paris in the late 1820s, he brought with him some daguerreotypes. His artist friends, on being shown these first photographs, lamented, 'Our profession is gone'; but Turner, more sanguine, answered 'We shall only go about the country with a box like a tinker, instead of a portfolio under our arm'. In the event, neither prediction has proved exactly right. Not everyone turned in their palette for a Kodak, nor were visual artists reduced to penury (or at least no more than before). One hundred and twenty years later, there are still painters, even figurative painters, at work in this country.

'Flourishing' is perhaps not the word to use for an activity that for decades now has almost always been against the tide, out of fashion, mildly disapproved of by the powers that be. But, in that period, several British figurative artists have become world famous: Francis Bacon, Henry Moore, Lucian Freud, Kitaj, David Hockney. Still more, perhaps, deserve to have international reputations – one thinks immediately of Frank Auerbach, Leon Kossoff, Euan Uglow, and there are several more. A new crop of figurative artists appeared in the '80s – when figurative art was all the rage again – and more even in the '90s, by which time the pendulum had swung back strongly towards installation, video *e tutti quanti.*

This strange persistence of figurative art – not just in Britain, but especially strongly here – requires an explanation. Is it simply a post mortem effect, a folkloric continuance of old technology after its primary function has gone? Do people continue to paint pictures with paint and brush rather as a few crafty eccentrics carry on with the spinning-wheel, the hand-loom, and the scythe?

There are many who would answer that question, 'Yes – figurative painting, perhaps any painting these days, is exactly like that.' The anti-painting camp argues essentially that the activity has become out-moded.

In his last year's Andrew Mellon lectures, Arthur Danto argued that the history of art divides into four periods. Up to 1400 or so, the essential role of what we now call 'art' was to provide objects of religious veneration – not really what we call art at all. From the Italian Renaissance until the late 19th century, the object of western artists was simply to heighten mimetic realism to the maximum possible degree. He calls this the Vasarian narrative.

From Cézanne and the impressionists on, however, the vanguard of artists changed direction. Panicked by the advent of photography, or perhaps bored by the perfectly bland naturalism of the Salon, painters started to concentrate instead on the paint itself, rather than on what it was depicting.

From that point, an inexorable chain of logic led to the colour-field painting advocated by the late Clement Greenberg, and all black canvases of Ad Reinhardt. Then, the argument goes, art about flat paint was itself superseded by the conceptual progeny of Andy Warhol and Beuys, which brings us to the free for all of today.

True or false? Well, at this stage in the twentieth century – after the collapse of Marxism and other notable intellectual edifices – one is instinctively suspicious of inexorable historical laws. The Danto thesis is full of art historical holes (for example, it is very odd to claim that painters as weirdly stylised in their different ways as El Greco, Poussin and William Blake were simply in search of realism). None the less, there is enough substance in the charge to demand an answer. Something certainly has happened to figurative painting in the last century and a half. It has become rarer, and, it is often claimed – not least by figurative artists – more difficult to do. After all, what can a painting of a person contribute that a photograph, or video film, cannot?

I think there are several answers – and the fact that there are several helps explain the diverse appearance that figurative painting has these days. The first answer is that through painting and drawing the artist can break through to a different, perhaps more profound kind of truth about the real world. This is the reason why a number of important British figurative painters employ methods that are both immensely effortful, and, also, viewed from outside, notably eccentric. In the old days, there was such a thing as a received technique. Now virtually every important artist invents a personal method, impossibly ill-adapted to anyone else.

The second answer, to which I shall return below, is that painting allows the artist to show things that don't exist at all in the world – in other words to create imagery out of thin air, out of his or her imagination or tell a story. Those tasks were of course – contrary to the Danto thesis – exactly what many artists were engaged upon between the Italian Renaissance and the birth of Impressionism – and after that.

Photography is not the ultimate – or the only – way of depicting the world; on the contrary, it's complete assendency would represent a dulling down, a destruction of imaginative diversity.

But let's take the first case first – the kind of painters who try to go deeper into our experience of reality, of the world around us. Leon Kossoff, writing about Frank Auerbach's drawings, once said, 'Drawing is not a mysterious activity. Drawing is making an image which expresses commitment and involvement. This only comes after seemingly endless activity before the model or subject, rejecting time and time again ideas which are possible to preconceive. And, whether by scraping off or rubbing down, it is always beginning again, making new images, destroying images that lie, discarding images that are dead.'

It is this effort more than any stylistic bond, that connects a group of artists including Kossoff himself, Frank Auerbach, Lucian Freud and Euan Uglow. This is the core of the so-called 'school of London' – though one might say that they were linked as much by affinities with the Swiss Parisian artist, Giacometti. It was Giacometti who, after a surrealist youth, began again to work from life in the belief that his true vocation was to paint and sculpt the world around him in the conviction that this was not easy – like a camera image – but difficult to the point of impossibility. In different ways, and with very different results, all the artists listed above adhere to these beliefs.

'I could splodge off something in three-quarters of an hour', Uglow said recently, 'But it wouldn't mean anything to me. It's only after a certain amount of time that you really understand a form and find a way of sticking it down as a flat shape. But one finishes each picture in despair. Ten years later I may feel, oh well, that's not bad'. Uglow observes the same model, rigorously posed in precisely the same position, his own viewpoint locked by horizontal and vertical plumb lines, for years on end.

Freud is also a notoriously snail-like executant, although in recent years he appears to have speeded up a little. Kossoff and Auerbach – like the late Francis Bacon – on the other hand, often paint extremely rapidly, but the resulting image is almost always scraped off, and the process is repeated 'time and again', 'seemingly endlessly' – so that a given painting may take as long to complete as an Uglow or Freud. Underlying all these procedures is the belief, articulated in various ways, that it is possible through intense effort to break through into a genuinely, fresh, true, unclichéd image.

So figurative painting of this type – trying to transmit what is really there – has built into it the precariousness and elusiveness of our sense of reality. That is one reason why Uglow or Freud seem to grope where Piero della Francesca or Titian worked with glorious certainty. It is true that many of the most important figurative painters are strongly aware of tradition. Exhibitions such as the Poussin and Cézanne shows in London in recent years are crucial events for them, necessitating innumerable, even daily visits. Painting, as Frank Auerbach once remarked, is a cultured activity – without the benchmarks of Velazquez, and Poussin, Rubens and Cézanne, 'We'd be floundering'. But one kind of historical inevitability applies: it is impossible to work today exactly like an old master, simply because today's artist automatically thinks like a late 20th century, not a 15th or 17th century, person. The awkwardness, the sense of effort, the occasional clumsiness are not signs of failure, but marks of truth.

Part of the process, for all of these painters – but not for the late Francis Bacon – is the practice of working directly from a model. That is, painting not what one remembers, or knows, or imagines, but closely examining a person who is actually in front of the easel. By such scrutiny more truth, a more telling living image, can be created. Lucian Freud once talked about wishing to paint not a picture of a person, but the person himself.

A number of younger artists continue to work from life, notably Celia Paul, Jenny Saville, Alison Watt, and Ishbel Myerscough. The last two – who are both graduates of Glasgow School of Art – have often taken themselves as models (as has Freud himself). Paul paints, again and again, members of her family circle, particularly her mother. In some cases – particularly in the work of Paul – there is a hint of the almost psychic closeness between painter and model that Freud manages to attain. Tai-Shan Schierenberg deploys a looser technique than any of the above, but his approach is fundamentally similar – in fact, at times, extremely Freudian.

In the work of all of these artists there is an attempt to produce an image of a specific human being that is more weighty, both psychologically and physically, than a photographic portrait or nude, more vividly there. In a number of paintings, Saville particularly – like Freud – has painted models who are themselves mountainous in physique. In the nudes she exhibited a few years ago of gigantic naked woman, massive to start with and painted over life-size, she attained a sort of punk baroque. Myerscough too has produced images of bodies immensely non-standard, so to speak, utterly unidealised, festooned with wrinkles, bulges and tattoos.

The specific reality of the individual face and body, seen in a completely illusionless way that comes from long, long hours of work from life – this continues to be an objective of figurative painting. There is a determined literalness about work of this kind – an absolute refusal of all rhetorical flourishes and imaginative softening – that in the work of Freud himself paradoxically produces an effect of revelation. He paints so insistently exactly what he sees before him that we the viewers suddenly see much more, sometimes much deeper, than our usual half attentive glance, blunted by boredom or anxiety, allows. And it is something that painting can do better, or at least differently, than photography. John Minton was photographed brilliantly on several occasions, most memorable by John Deacon. But the Freud portrait is more profound, more compelling – perhaps because of the sheer intensity of the looking and working that went into it.

Freud has famously said that he wants his paint to work as flesh, and there he touches on one of the basic facts in the history of oil painting ('flesh was the real reason oil painting was invented' said De Kooning). Paint can give the human face and body far more presence and immediacy than any other known medium, because it is itself, oily, thick, flexible looking – an equivalent to skin that can be manipulated in endlessly varied ways by the painter.

There is a sense in which this current in contemporary painting – which might be dubbed the Freudian stare – runs parallel to other, quite different currents in contemporary art. This is painting of the human figure shorn much more radically of the pattern-book idealism of the ancient Greeks than that of, say, Matisse or, in one mood, Picasso. On the other hand, it is much less transmuted by subjective emotion than Picasso, in other moods, or Beckmann and the expressionists.

It is a hard look at what is actually there – mapped in the case of Freud himself, it sometimes seems, inch by inch. As such it has some affinities with an artist such as Damien Hirst, who simply serves up chunks of what is really there. Whether painting or shop-window displays of regalia are in fact more moving and revealing, only the judgement of time will tell. Also, the disenchanted, bare, sometimes downright seedy setting of so much contemporary figurative art – the bare boards, the plaster, the rawness of it – has a similar mood to much work produced by the amorphous group collectively known as the *Young British Artists.*

There are however other imperatives that painting carries with it – among them, the need to find a formal design that snaps together as tightly as a lock. It is the search for that which seems to be behind the endless working and reworking of Kossoff and Auerbach, for example. The quest is for a formal lock that will catch and preserve not only the subject but the artist's experience of the subject. And that, to make the matter yet more arduous, is a moving target. 'Nothing', Kossoff once wrote, 'Is ever the same. Every time the model sits everything has changed. You have changed, she has changed. The light has changed, the balance has changed.' Those are the kind of imponderables that make figurative painting both so difficult, and so rewarding when someone manages to trap this flux in paint.

Implicit in figurative art in the tradition of Giacometti, Freud and Bacon is the belief that photography is not the arbiter of visual truth. This is a question that David Hockney, a very different kind of artist to those discussed above, has tackled head on. We have, he feels 'a naive belief in the photograph as objective reality. The photograph in its single form is the end of a way of seeing, not a beginning, it is the last of the Renaissance way of looking, and as such it should be attacked more than it is'.

He has developed these ideas in his book, 'That's the Way I See It', and they all lie behind all of his work since the late '70's. This has taken a bewildering variety of forms including a sort of landscape-based abstraction and photo-collage. But the photo-pieces – many shots of a subject from different viewpoints – were ways of proving that the monocular vision of the lens told only a very partial kind of truth. While his semi-abstracts, and recent flower-studies and portraits all seem dedicated to showing that painting can give a more vivid experience of space than the photograph.

This preoccupation with space is the other half of the Giacomettian inheritance. Giacometti's subject was the fragility of the human being in the mysterious vastness of space. Some artists who work from life today are preoccupied with the fragility, individuality, and sheer existence of their human subject. Others are more obsessed by space. Another – quite different – example is John Wonnacott, an artist who was influenced early on by Giacometti, but developed from that into an obsession with panoramic wide-angle perspective. His sweeping spaces contain much more than we actually see, or are aware of seeing at a single glance. But they convey the excitement, the exhilaration, and also the sheer oddity of being in, and looking at, the immensity of light, and air and things around us.

A literal transcription of optical reality is impossible, as Wonnacott – and doubtless all the painters whose work is in this exhibition – are well aware. No human gaze will take in the wide-angle views that Wonnacott loves to paint, let alone the wild perspectival distortions of objects pulled about on the edges. But these furnish him with a world to explore, and to make formal sense of, together with an equivalent to a certain way of looking. Indeed, a large amount of painting in the last half century has attempted to pin down a certain way of seeing and give it a durable formal shape – not just British figurative painting but also for example, the work of De Kooning who talked of finding his content in 'slipping glimpses'. For that matter, it has been part of the aim of much apparently abstract art. But it too is something that photography cannot aspire to do, because the camera can only see in one way – or at most, a limited number of ways, in focus, out of focus, sharp, soft, high contrast, low contrast, and so on.

There is a great difference between the way that Wonnacott works, and the method of John Lessore, an artist with whom he worked closely in the life room at Norwich School of Art. The latter works from observations transmitted through drawings, and arranged into compositions. His work is thus a meditation on the memory of an experience, the final work perhaps being completed, after innumerable adjustments, years after the initial impulse. This is obviously a very different matter from working directly from the model (something that Lessore does only occasionally). The emotional tone of his work is correspondingly different – gentle, calm, contemplative.

Here we have an intermediary stage between working life, and working from imagination. There are in fact a large number of steps on that journey. Many artists paint the world around them, but in a way that is far from literal. Carel Weight, the doyen of British figurative painters, has for many years been painting his imaginative fantasies set in utterly mundane surroundings. In Weight's work, a ghost may materialise in a Fulham street, an angel hover above a South London park. A throng of Ensor-like grotesques float down from the sky. But the stage, so to speak, of his imaginative theatre is a closely observed, grimy run-down London of yellow Victorian brick and bay-windowed houses.

R B Kitaj – once like Hockney, misleadingly dubbed a pop artist – also straddles this divide, in a different way. Kitaj has produced a great deal of work from life, particularly a group of steamily erotic nudes from the '70s and early '80s. But the bulk of his work from first to last is made up of complex painted fictions and allegories, mingling references to art, literature, history and Kitaj's own life, into which from time to time a real person, such as Hockney, may intrude.

The Scottish trio of Peter Howson, Ken Currie and Jock McFadyen are after a certain harsh contemporary reality which is just as raw and disenchanted as the bare boards and armpits of some work done these days directly from the model. McFadyen takes to regions inhabited by a hard-drinking, tattoo-splattered underclass; Howson's work even before his traumatic spell as a war artist in Bosnia focused obsessively on the violence of over-muscled, under-civilised men.

Ray Richardson specialises so to speak in a Cockney version of this school of grotesque social reportage. His world is not quite so poverty-stricken, drink-sodden and derelict as Howson's Glaswegian milieu; it is more specifically criminal, a hellish darkly amusing place of sharp designer suits, smart cars and killer dogs.

There may be an original, perhaps horrific, observation – Howson in Bosnia for example did numerous rapid drawings on the spot – but the final result is marked by expressionist and caricatural stylisation (caricature, far from being solely the domain of cartoonists, is one of the most powerful modes of the visual arts). For instance, Otto Dix, an artist of whom one is sometimes reminded by Howson, was essentially producing violent and shocking caricature both in his portraits and in his images of the First World War.

It is precisely the fact that these three painters make use of a variety of deadly serious (and in McFadyen's case, not so serious) caricature – that gives their work its popularist force. Caricature, of course, is beyond the normal range of photography – witness the fact that of an army of illustrators who used to be employed by the press, only the cartoonists have survived – though there is a photographic equivalent in photomontage (Michael Heath, for example, of the Spectator employs both).

Painters such as Ken Kiff and Eileen Cooper are scarcely giving us even a caricature of the human face and figure. Their people are closer to pictograms, graphic equivalents for human beings that have their own point. The fact that their world is schematic by the same token makes it universal, a place for epics and parables to unfold.

With the work of Paula Rego, for the most part, we have left the real world for her personal variety of disquieting painted fable (though some of the large female figures she has produced in recent years have the air of being worked from life). It would be possible, perhaps to stage one of Rego's vignettes using real people in costumes, carefully constructed sets, and so forth – indeed, photographer-artists such as Jeff Wall and Cindy Sherman do something very similar to that. Possibly the staged photograph is one direction in which the tradition of narrative painting might evolve. But the effect would certainly be very different from a Rego – or, to take the example of another painter who produces large, imaginative, narrative paintings, Ansel Krut.

The artificiality of a staged photograph, paradoxically, is greater. Such a photograph can't get away from being an ironic comment on the history of narrative painting, indicating how strange such scenes would appear in reality. It is very difficult for photography to lose its documentary look – that is what gives point to a Wall or a Sherman. But it is much easier for a painting to be accepted as dream or narrative. Also, with line and paint, the control of atmosphere, the possibility of pointed distortion, and formal clarity are greater. It will be interesting to see whether the carefully arranged – perhaps computer-aided – photograph really does supersede what used to be called the history painting, or whether it itself is merely a passing footnote in the history of narrative art.

There is also a note in Rego which is surreal, or perhaps, since that word carries so much historical luggage, it would be better to say concerned with dreams and reveries. She finds in the story of Peter Pan and nursery rhymes, psycho-sexual tension, incongruity and menace that match the mood of her own invented stories in paint. A similar dreamlike mood exists in the work of Stephen Chambers, whose figures and domestic paraphernalia float in space, weirdly disassociated from reality by the surrounding void – magical real inhabitants of what often looks like an abstract painting.

John Kirby combines surreal fantasy with the self dramatisation and examination which is a powerful motive in art of today from the self stripping of naked realist portraits, to the role playing of a photographic artist such as Cindy Sherman, or a video maker like Georgina Starr. It is apparent in the work of painters as diverse as Alison Watt, whose female figure is very often a mutated depiction of herself, longer in face and clumsier in demeanour. In Kirby's painting we may also encounter the artist himself, clad in his underpants, sprouting the wings of an angel. This is a fantasy that is not so fantastic since it bears an obvious relation to the artist's sexuality, and Catholic upbringing.

Surrealism is a mode that is clearly not beyond the reach of photography – as is evident from the work of Man Ray, among many others – but a painted fantasy and a photographic one are subtly different things. One can easily conceive of a photomontaged or computer-engineered equivalent to an image by, say, Magritte. But the feel of it would be quite different. Similarly, the fantasies of a Stephen Chambers, a Paula Rego, or an Andrzej Jackowski would not be themselves if they were photographed, not painted. Part of their individual dreamlike quality lies not in the imagery but in the touch and line. In the slightly naive air of Kirby's drawing, say, by photographic means, the result would certainly be different, possibly more banal.

Also essentially a fantasist, Peter Blake uses a beautifully naturalistic touch, and, one suspects, often a photographic basis, to paint things that simply couldn't happen – Renaissance Madonnas materialising among the skate-boarders and body-builders of Venice Beach, Los Angeles in one recent example. Again this clearly could be done by electronic manipulation of images. One could programme a Bellini into a snap of Muscle Beach. But it is hard to believe that the two would integrate so smoothly into a single zone of make-believe – (indeed, it is sometimes more than Blake himself can do to blend the two).

Photography and painting – and video for that matter – are not mutually exclusive. There is room for many media, including some new ones; indeed, we are often told – especially by those not keen on contemporary painting that it is a mistake to become hung up 'fetishistically' on a medium, particularly a sad old one such as paint.

Paint clearly is a very old technology for the depiction of the world around and inside us – some 30,000 years old, according to the cave paintings discovered in the South of France a year or two back. But old technology is not necessarily out-moded technology, as we have seen borne out in the last three years in the case of the printed book. The book is not as old as the painting, a mere five hundred years, but it was widely predicted to be about to be made obsolete by the CD-Rom and other electronic gismos. It didn't happen, though the CD-Rom is useful for certain purposes.

The same may well prove true of painting, which remains a unique, and uniquely flexible, versatile, way of engaging with visual reality. The way we see, it has sometimes been asserted, is the way we have been taught to see by artists. There is no set, photographic reality. What surrounds us is flux and chaos, the sense we make of it is in part at least the result of art that we have seen, digested and projected back upon the world. What we see when we look around us in a different way is thanks to

Cézanne, Constable or Matisse. That is one of the fundamental functions of art – not only figurative art, but abstract too. As David Hockney has written, if we are to carry on finding new ways of seeing, it must be through painting and drawing – because the lens cannot see in new ways, only in its own familiar, old ways.

Painting was always dead, Willem De Kooning once observed, 'I never let it bother me'. The painters whose work is on show in this exhibition would doubtless concur with that. The best of them make it live, and if it lives it will survive.

Martin Gayford

Plates

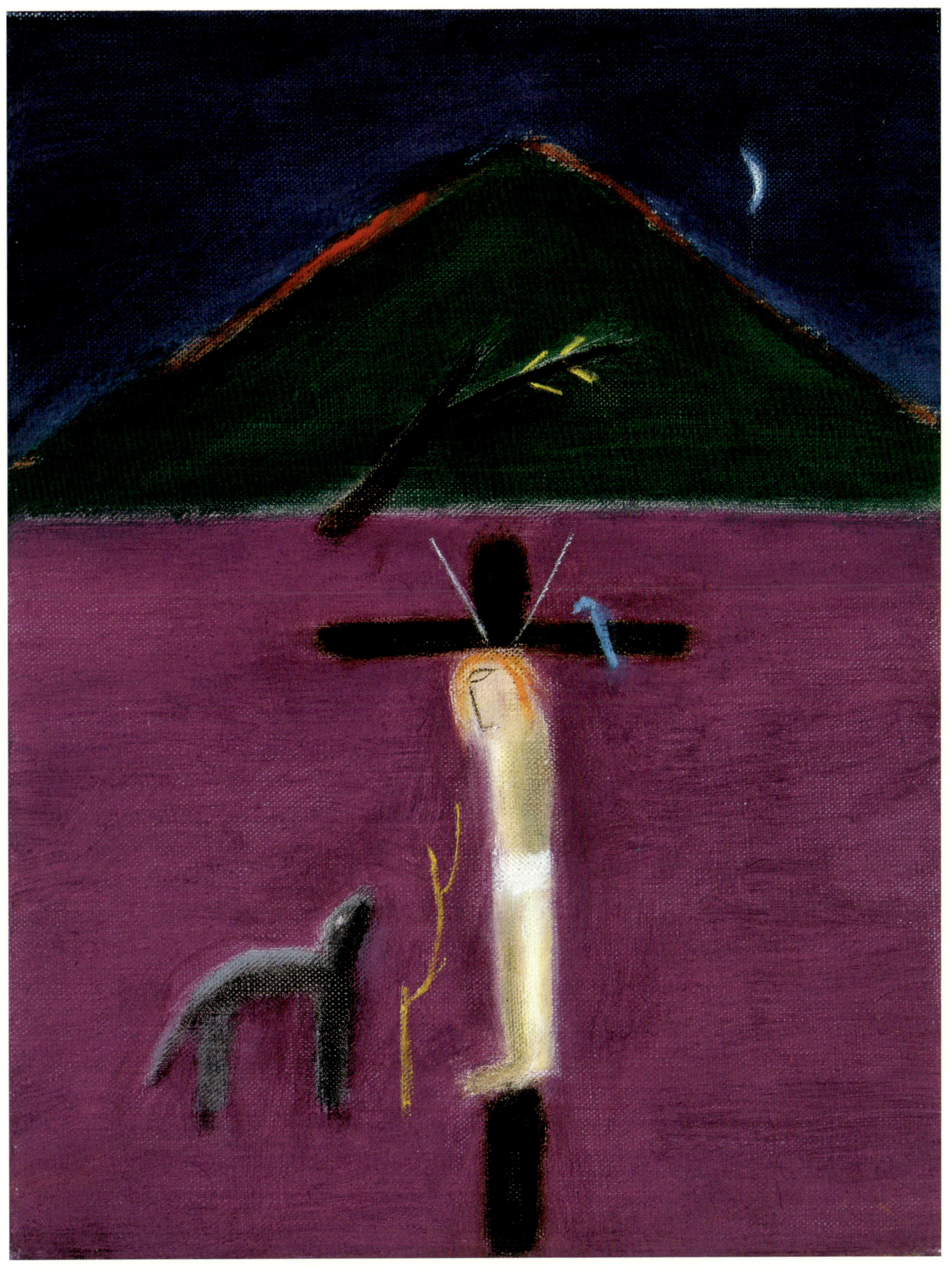

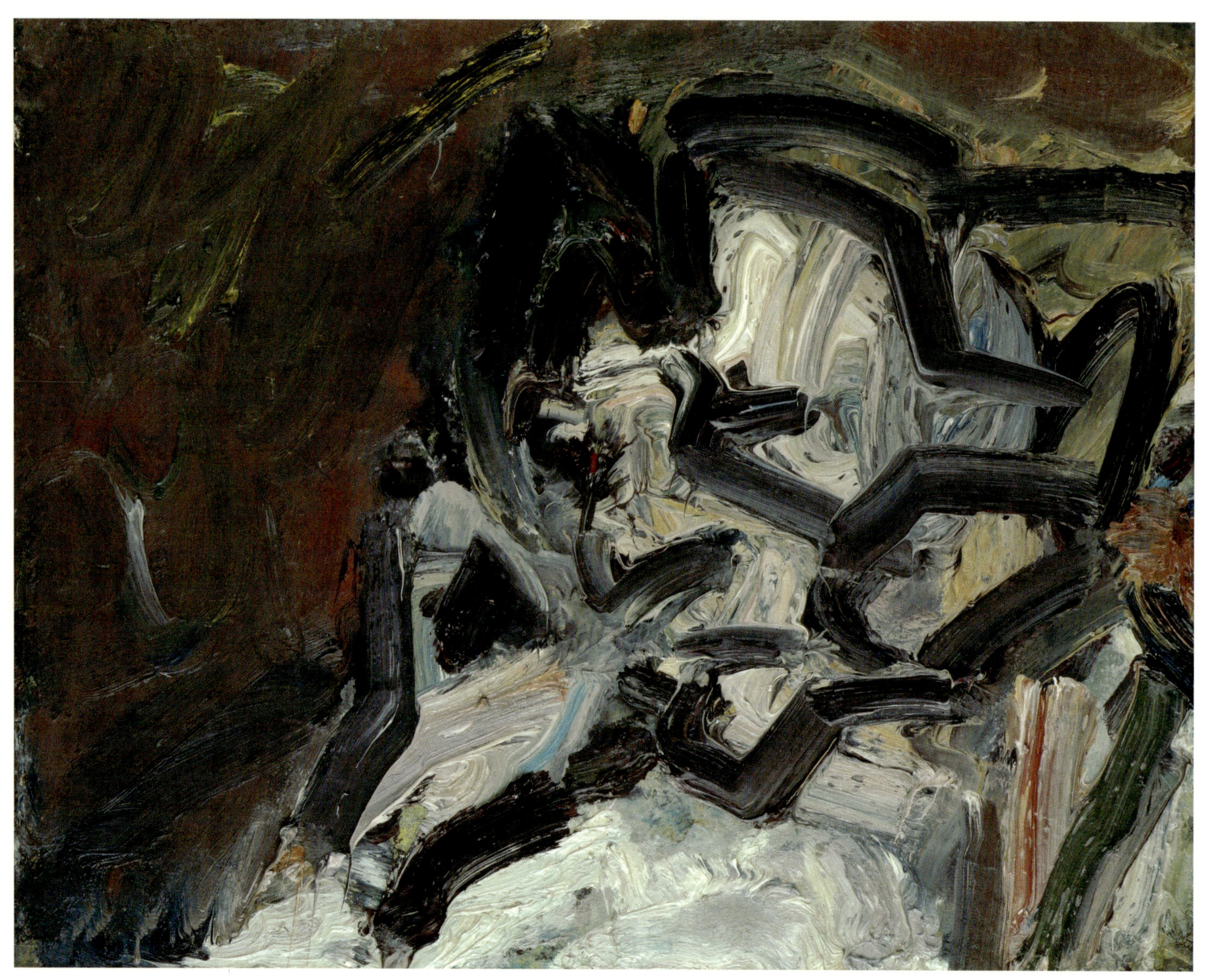

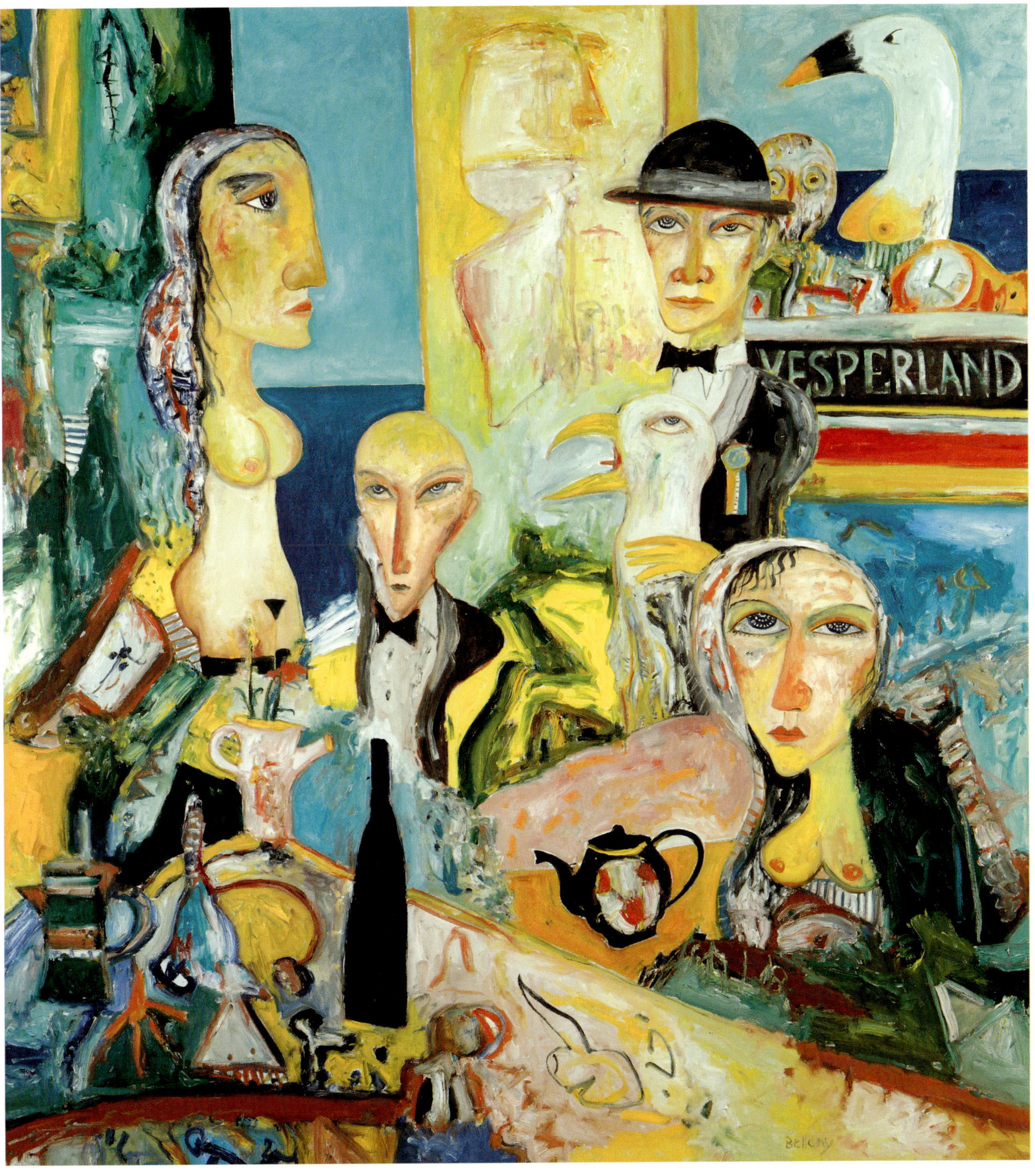
VESPERLAND
BELLANY

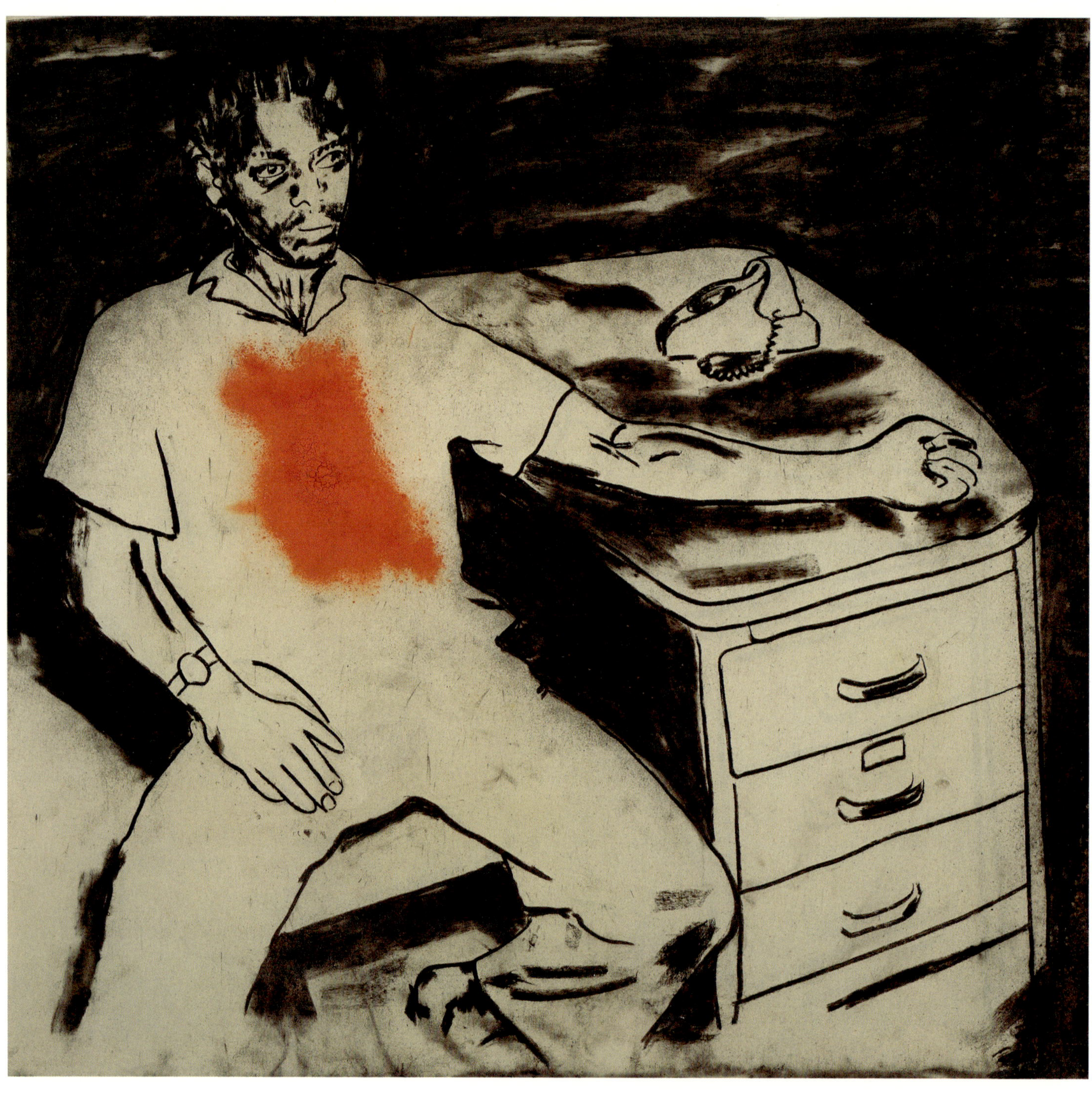

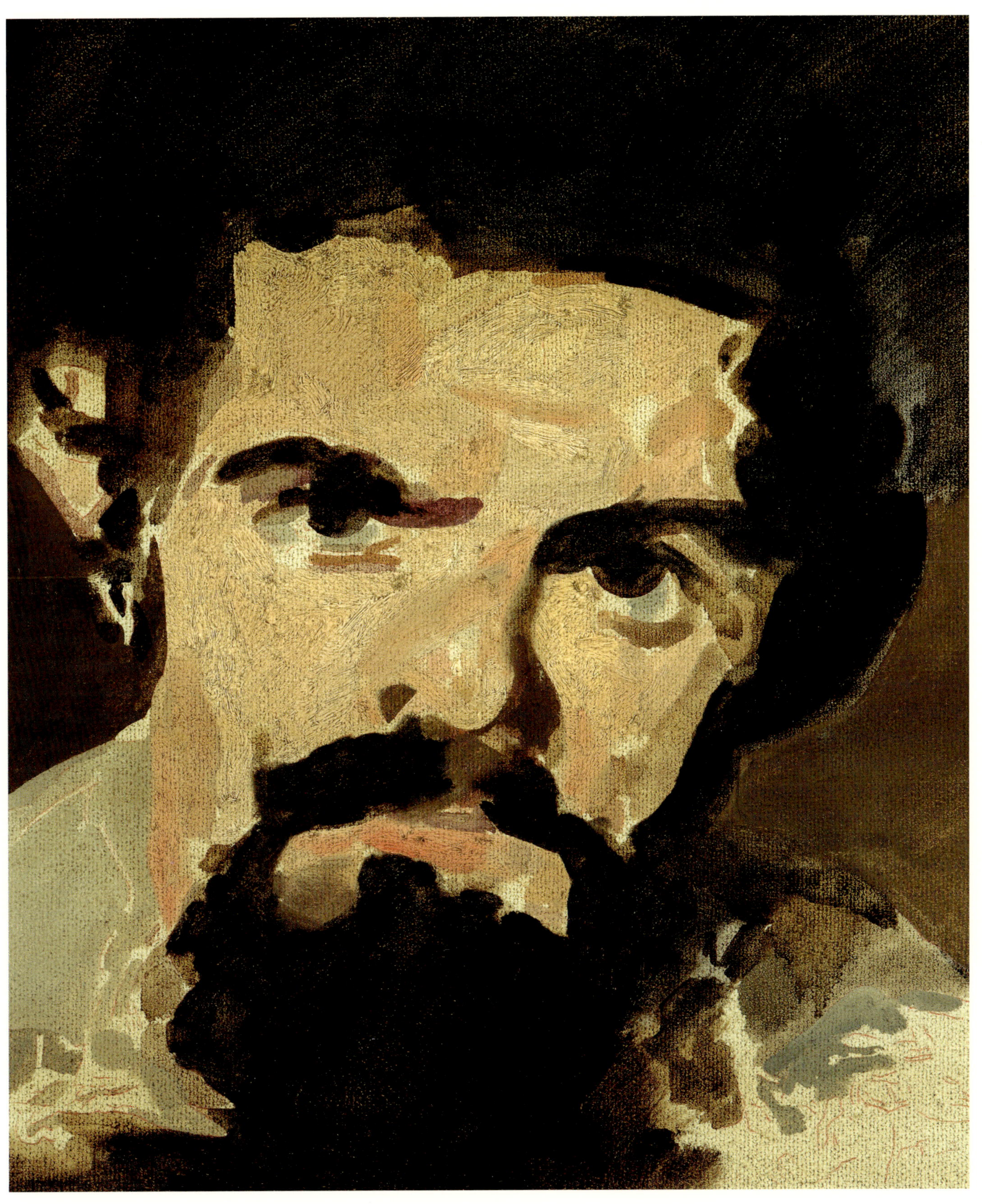

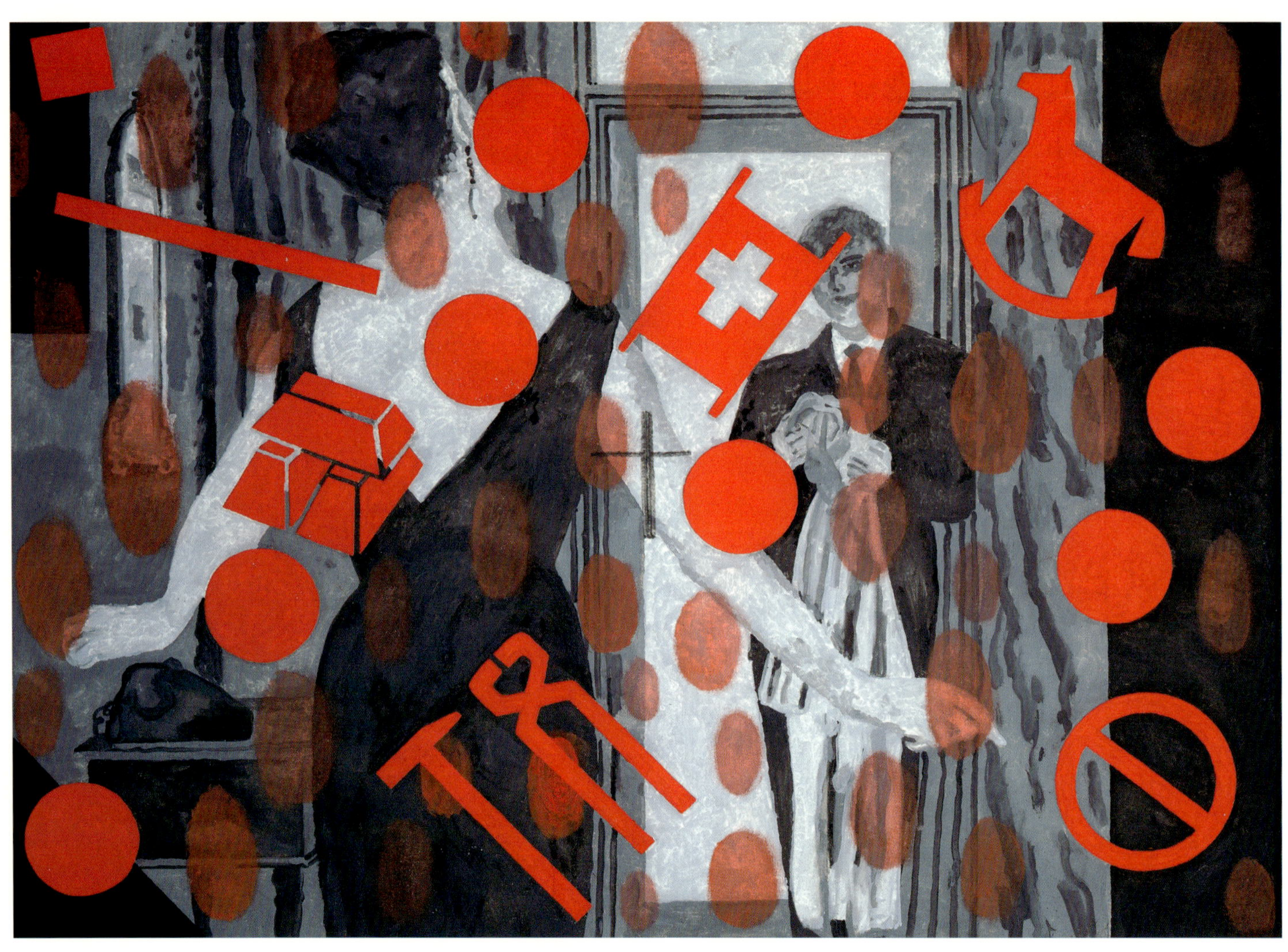

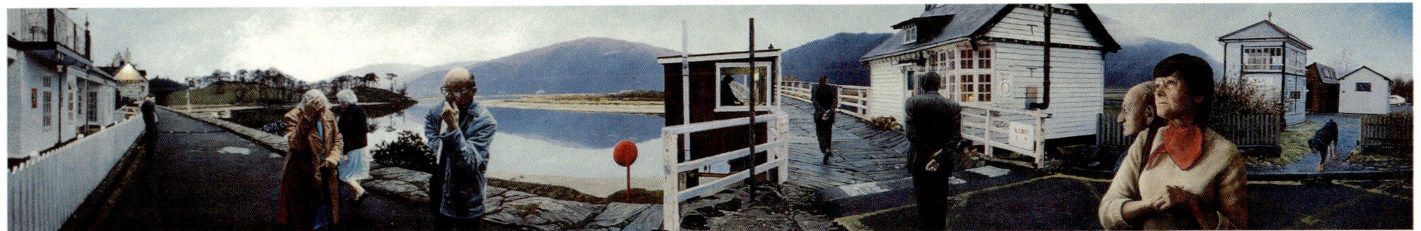

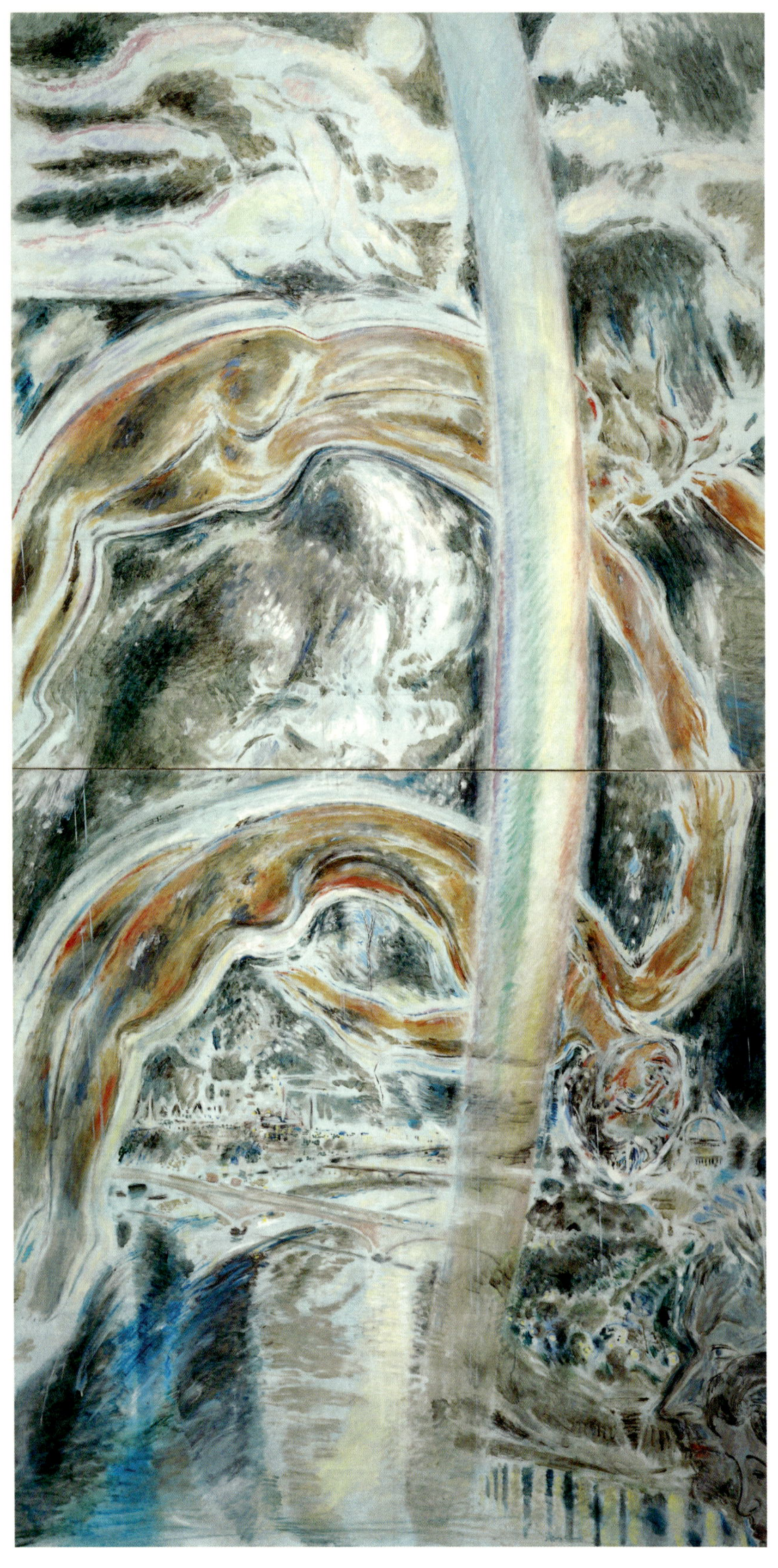

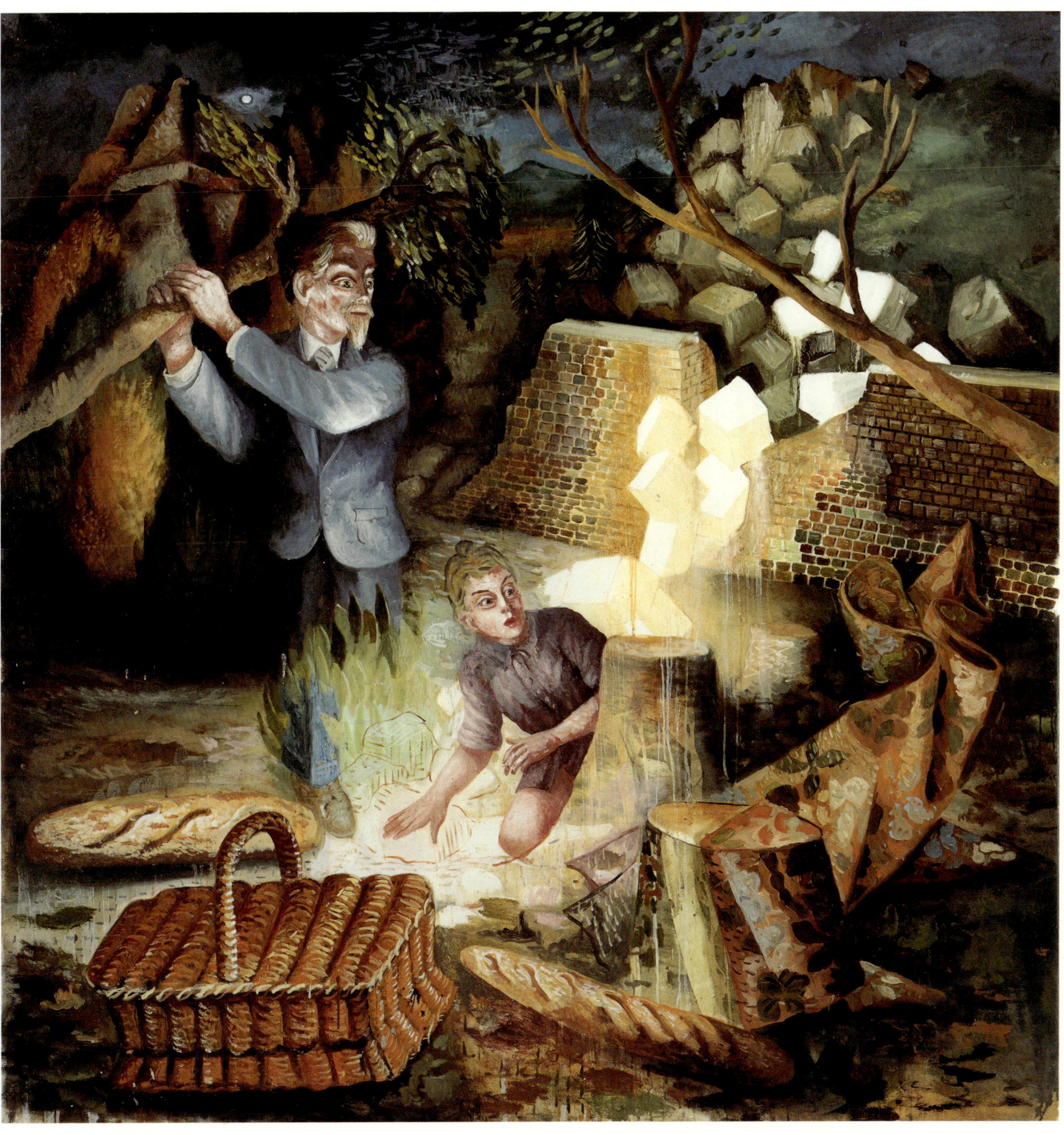

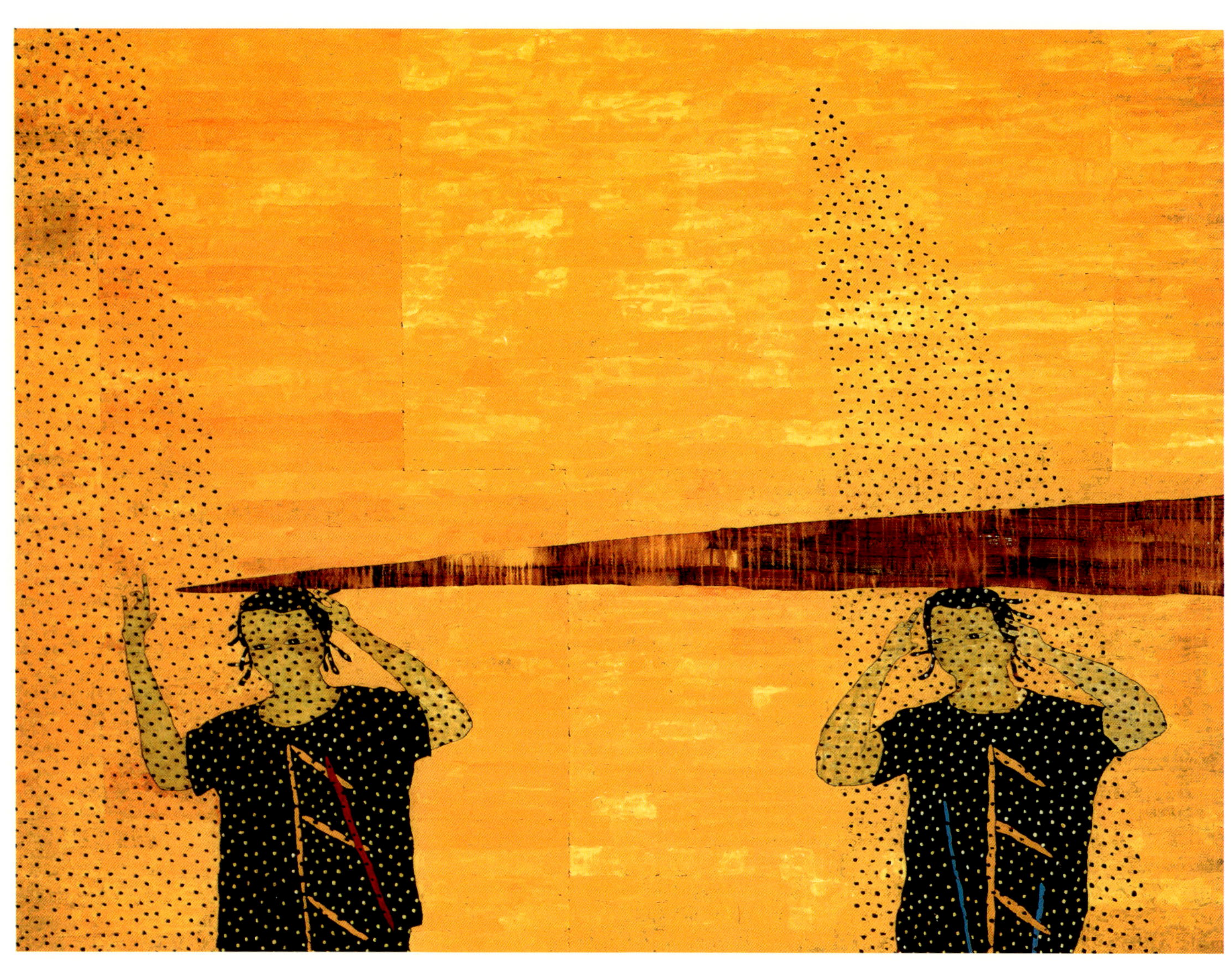

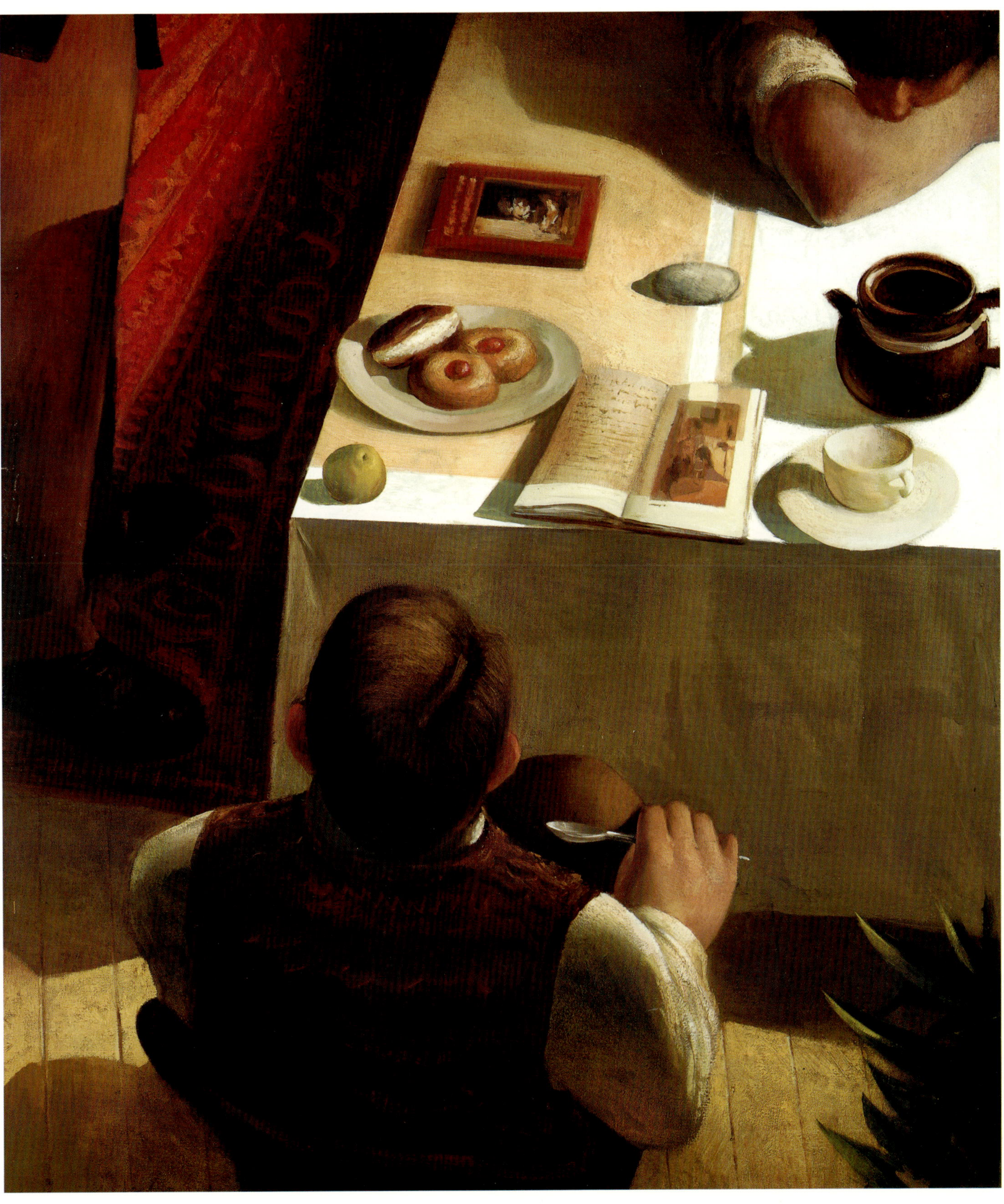

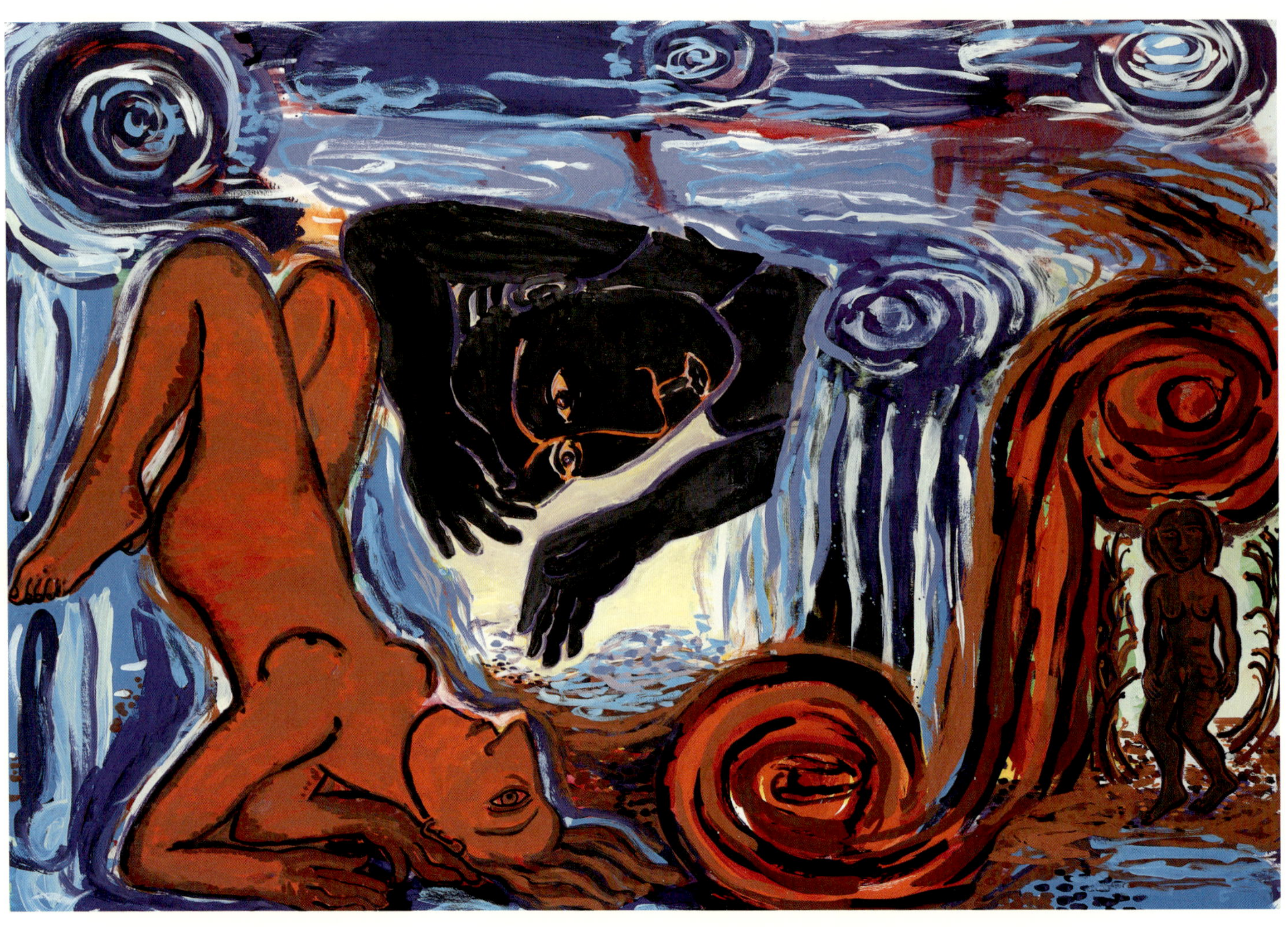

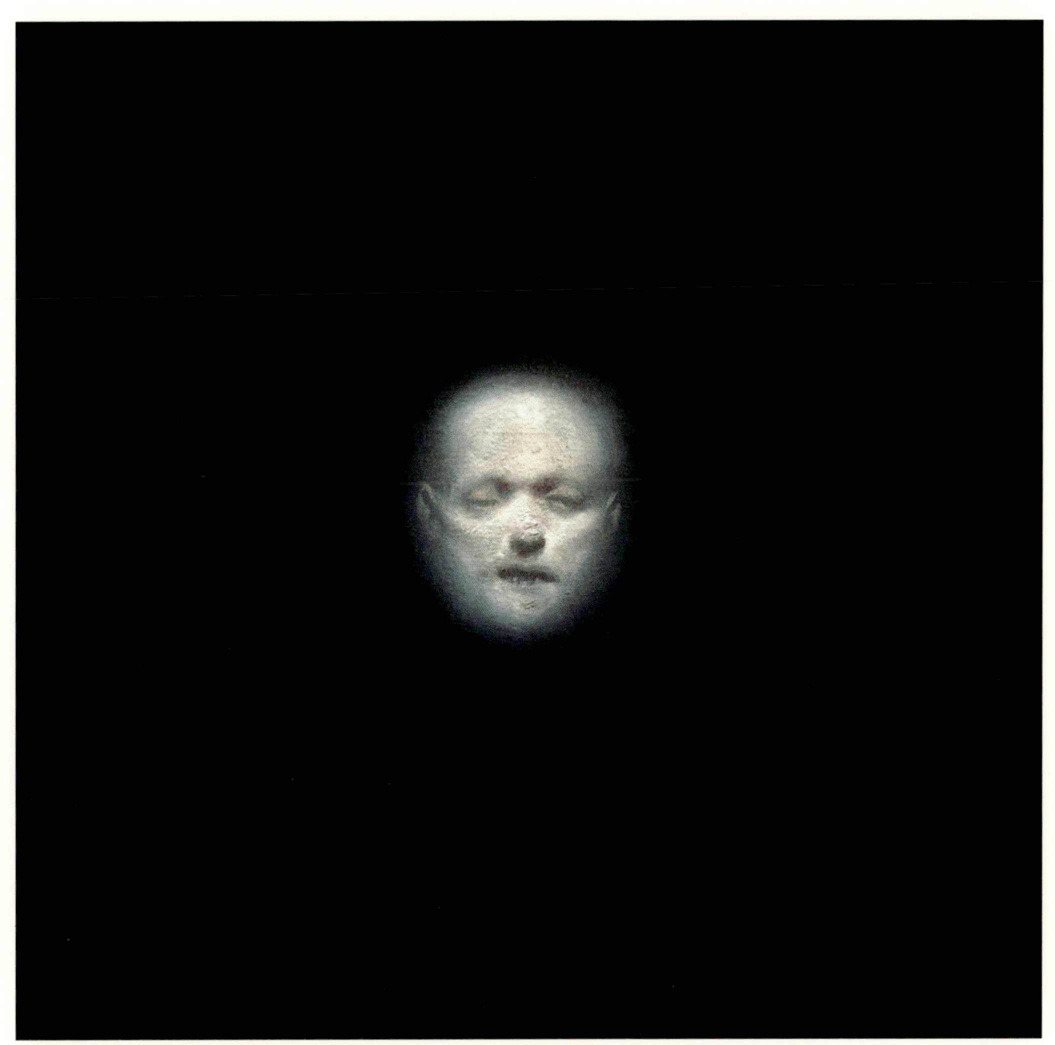

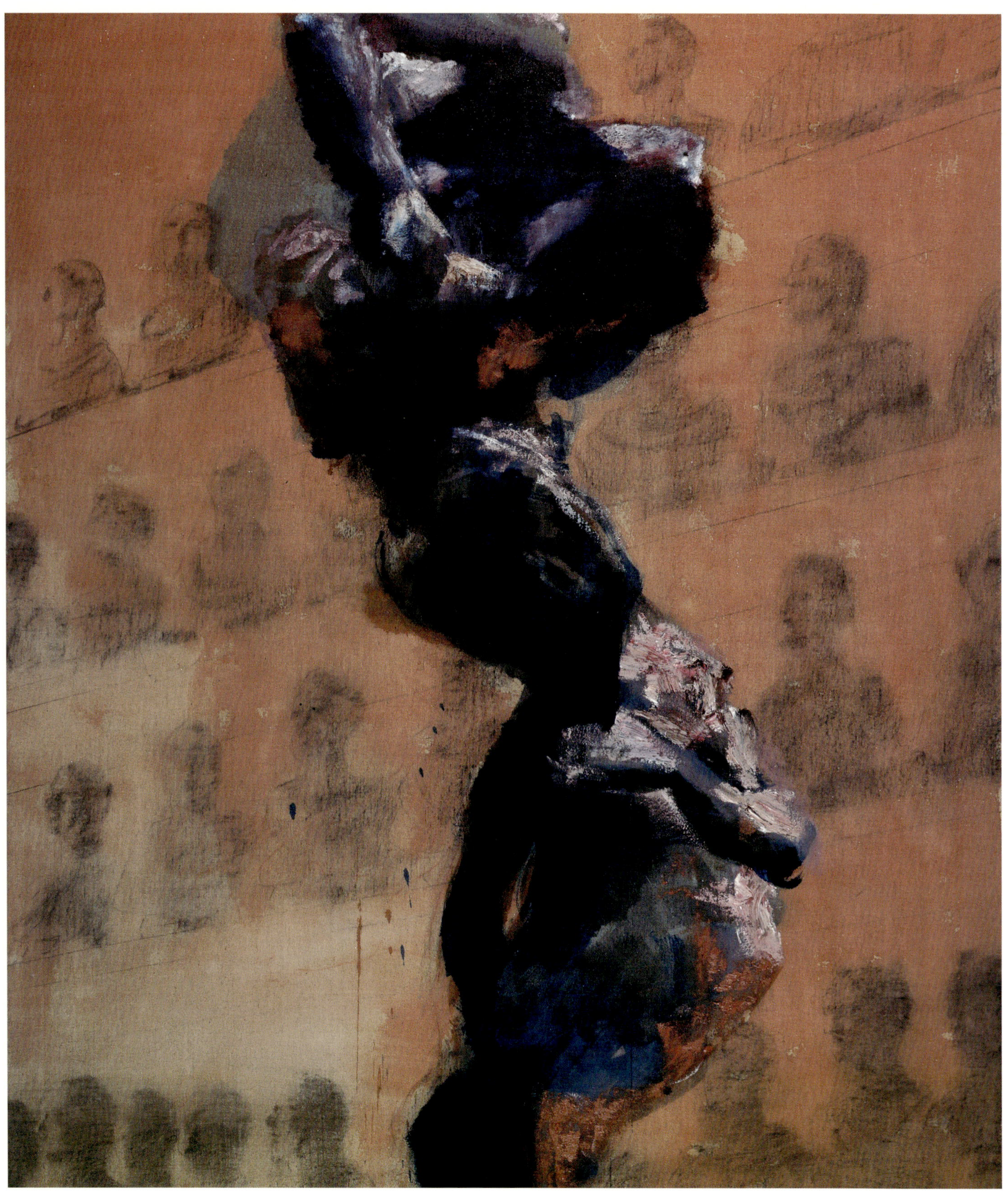

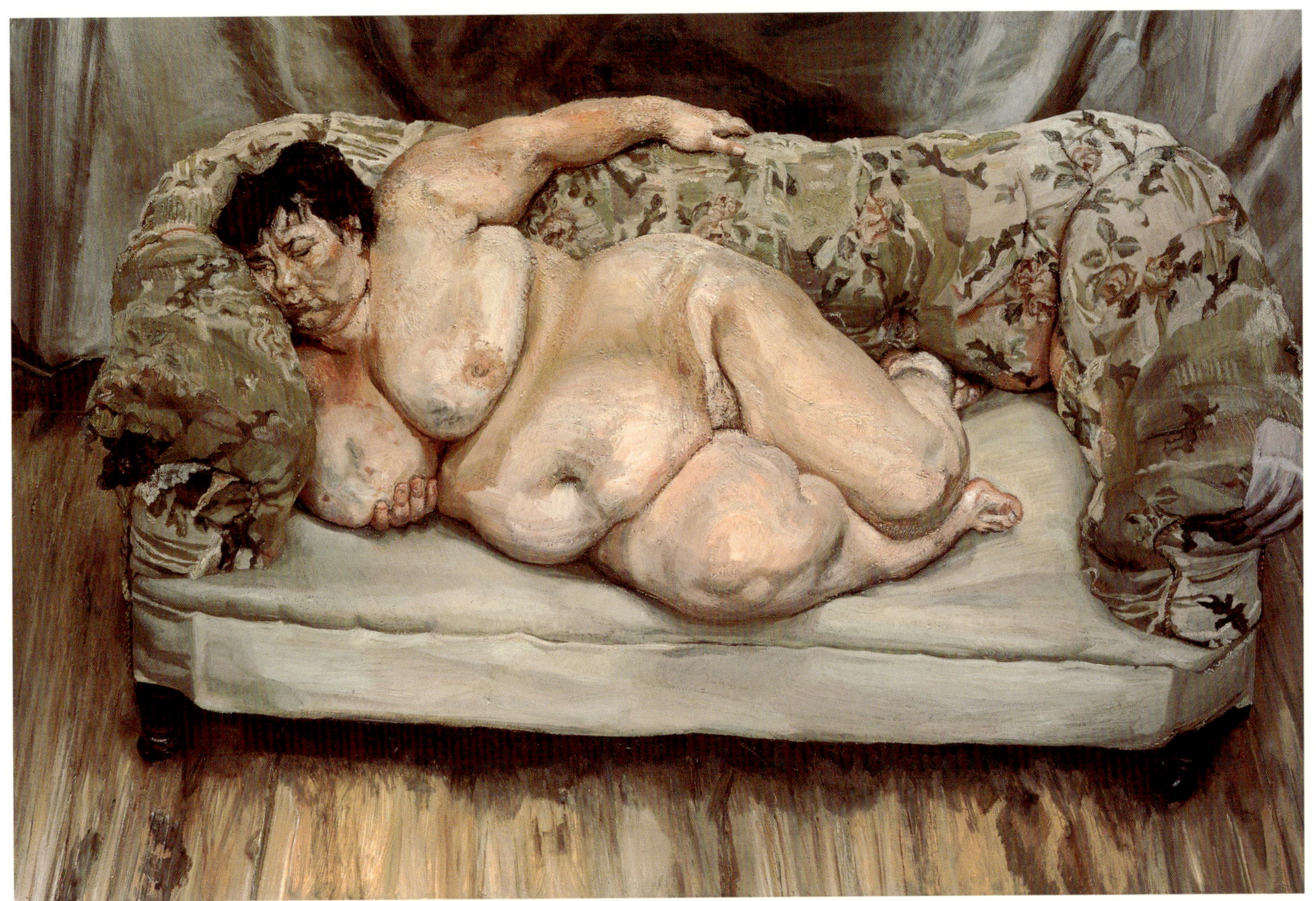

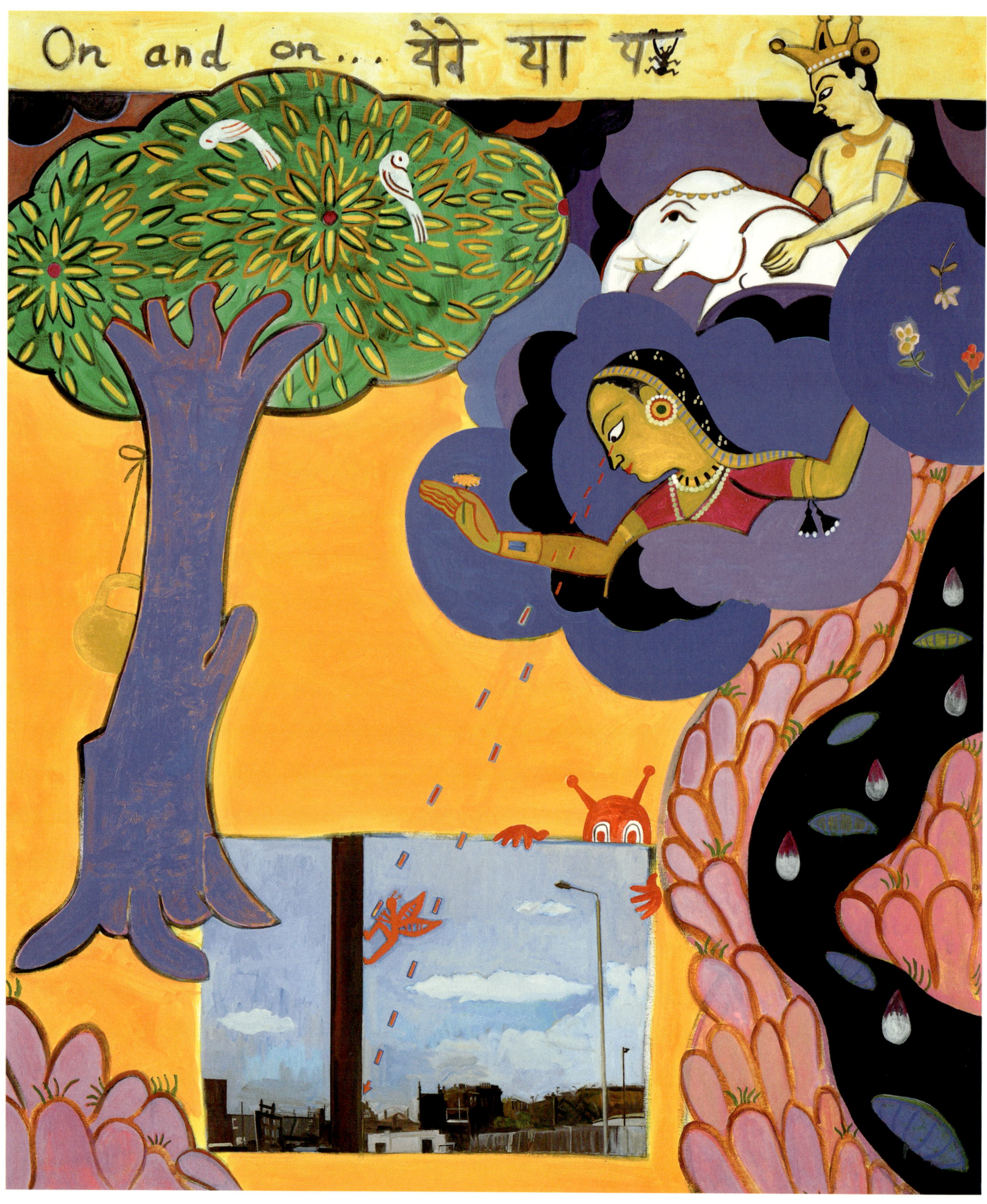
On and on...

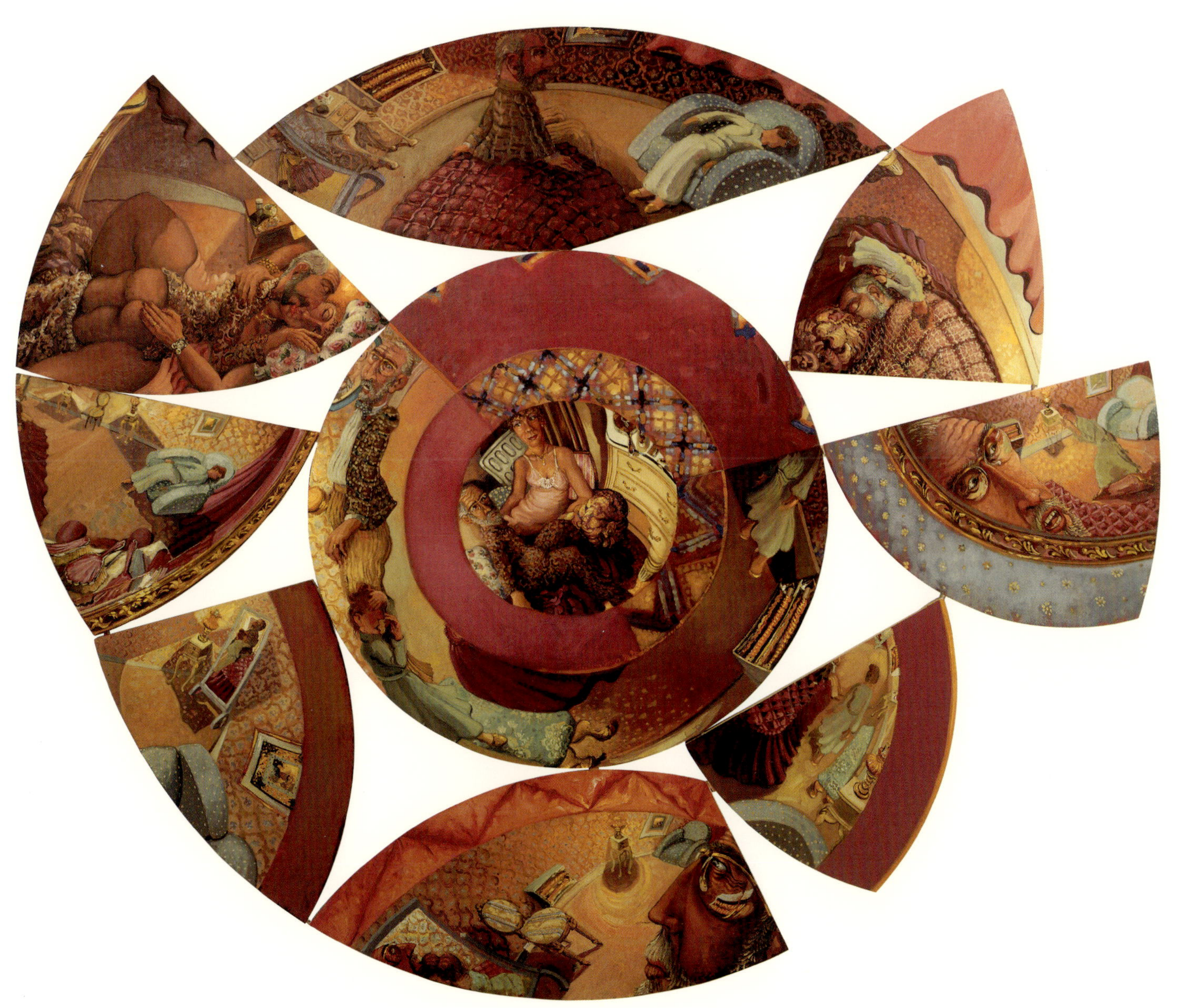

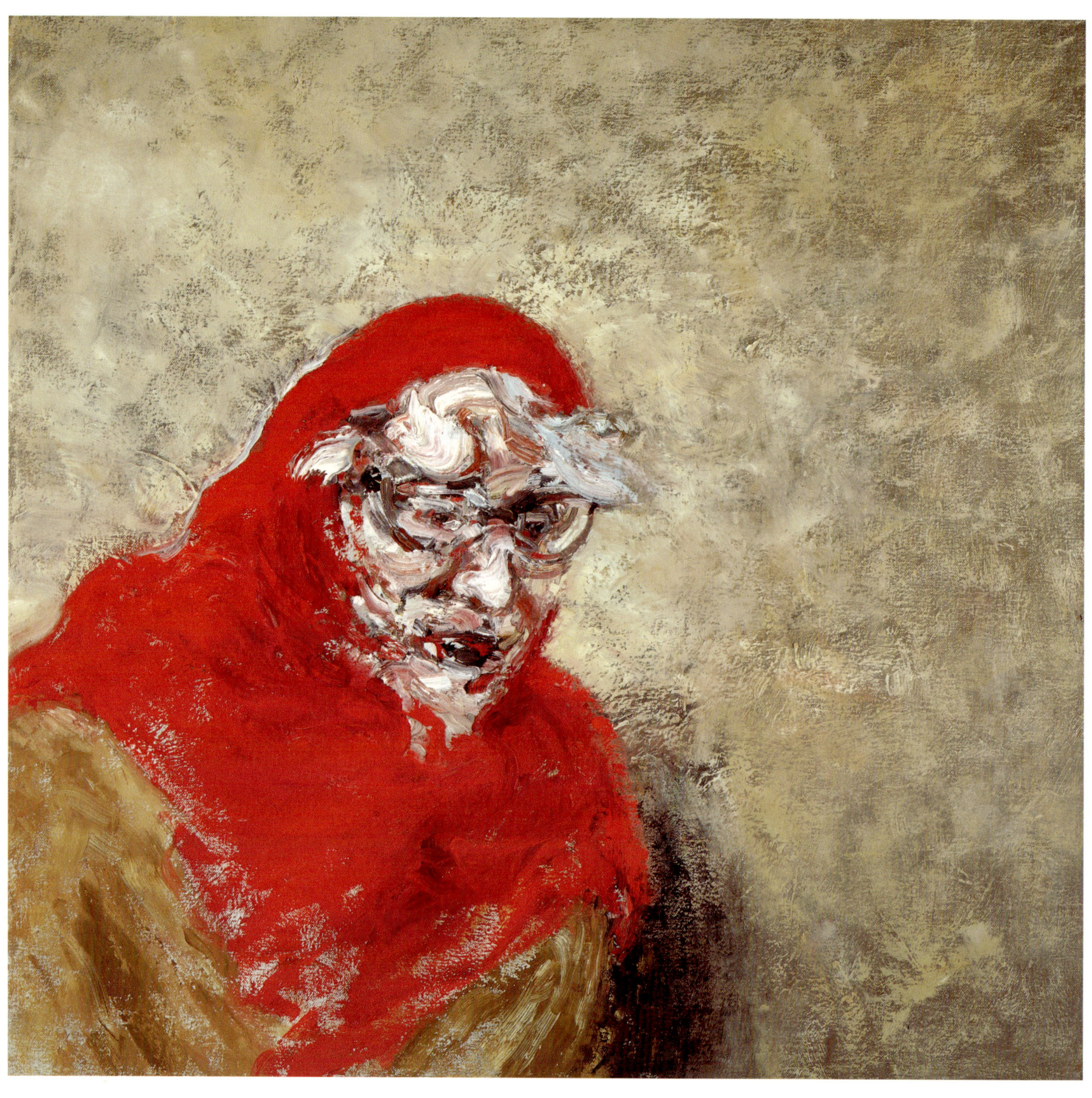

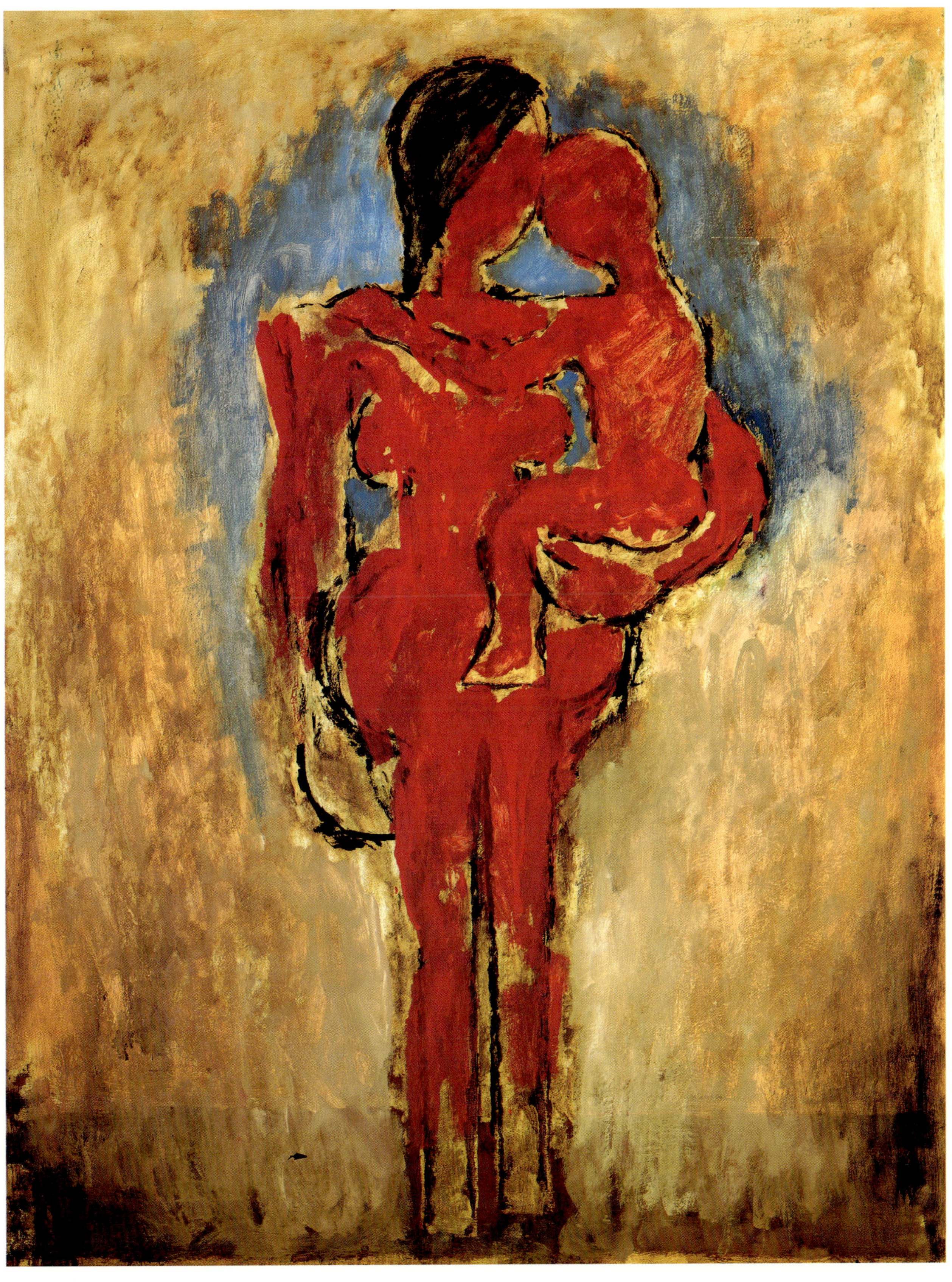

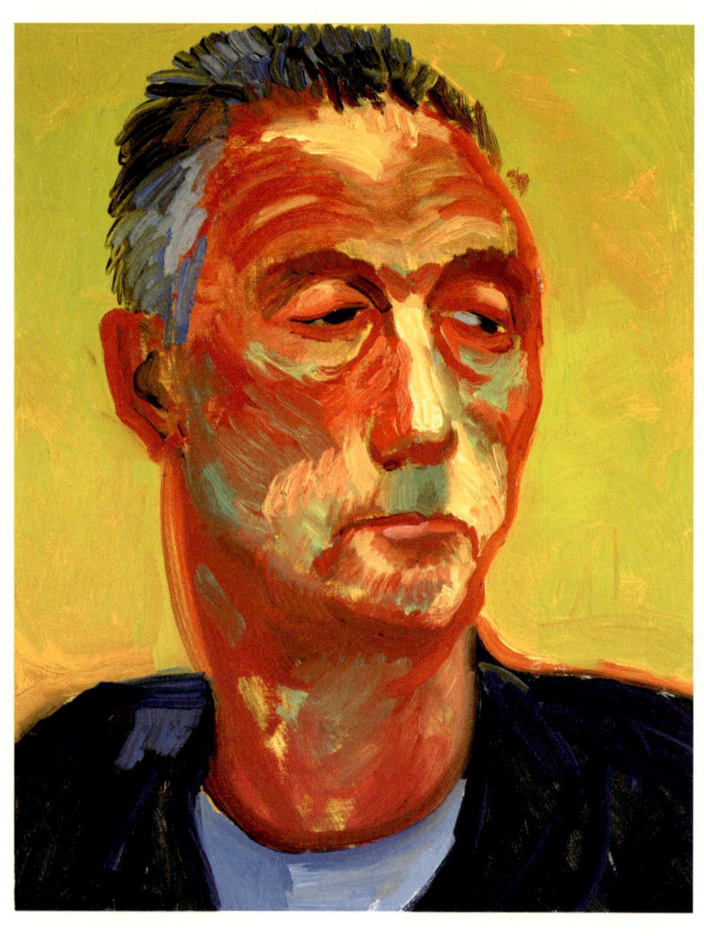

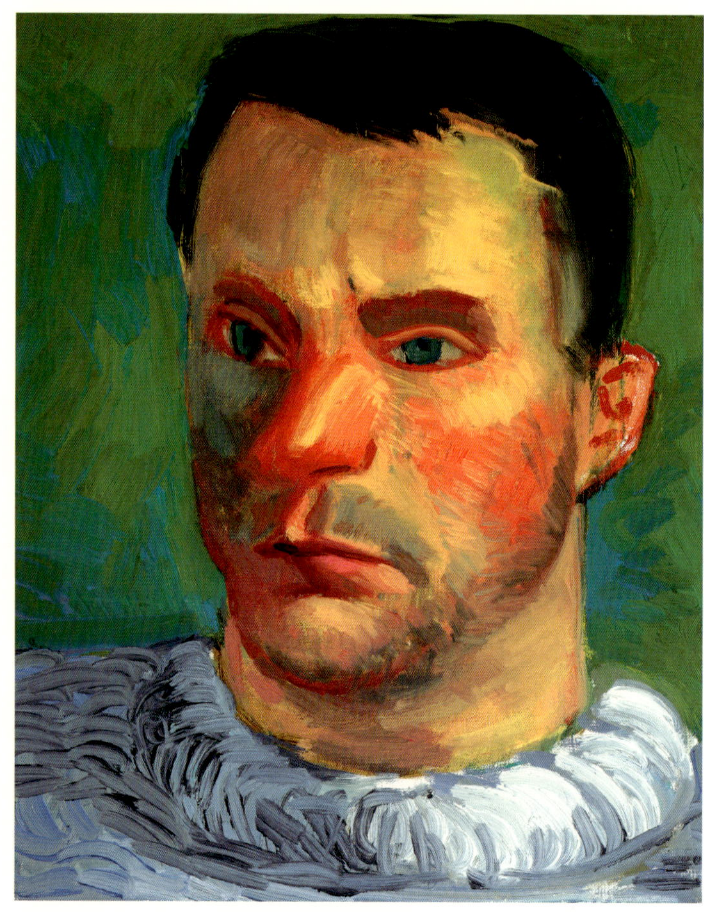

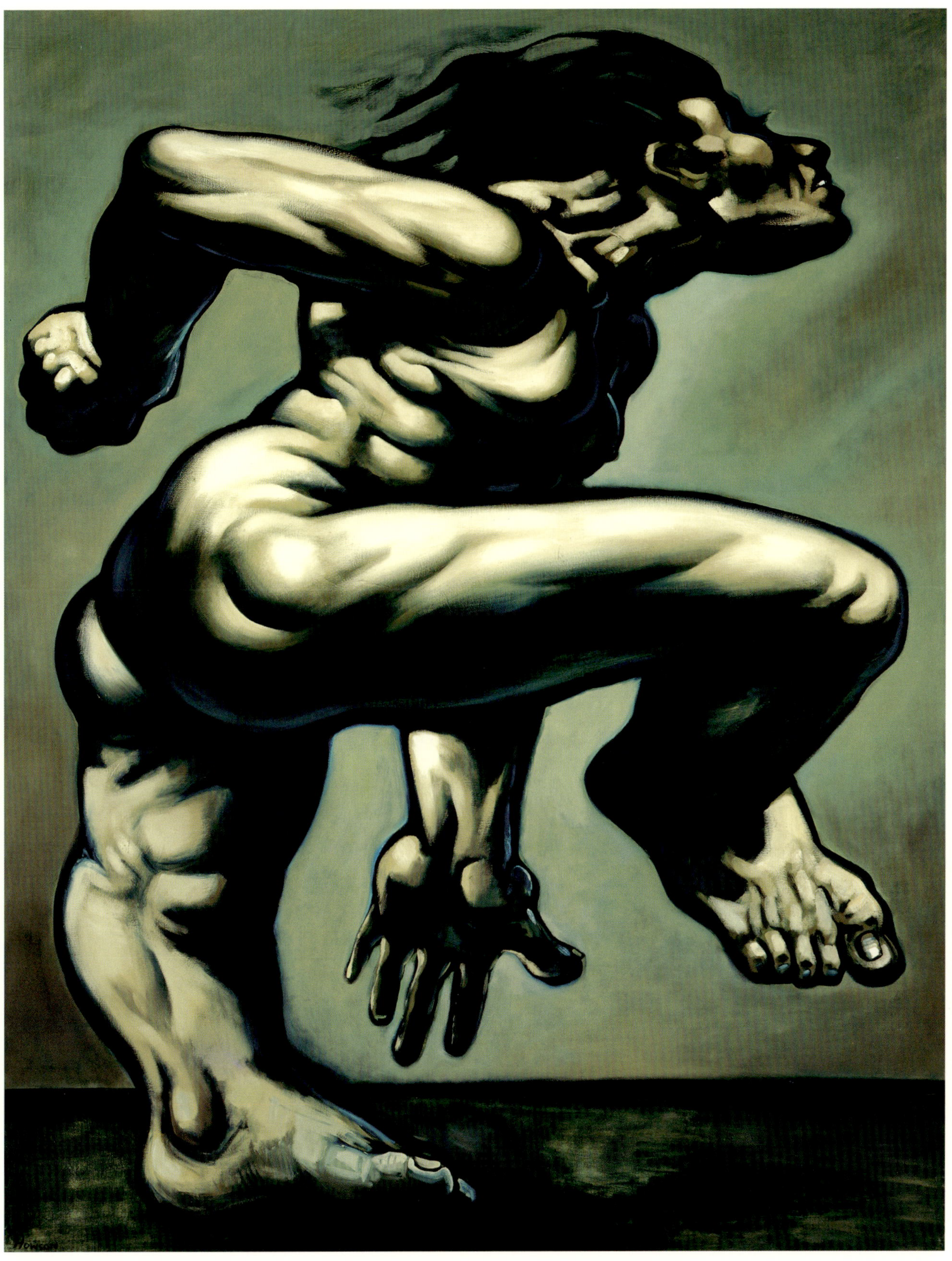

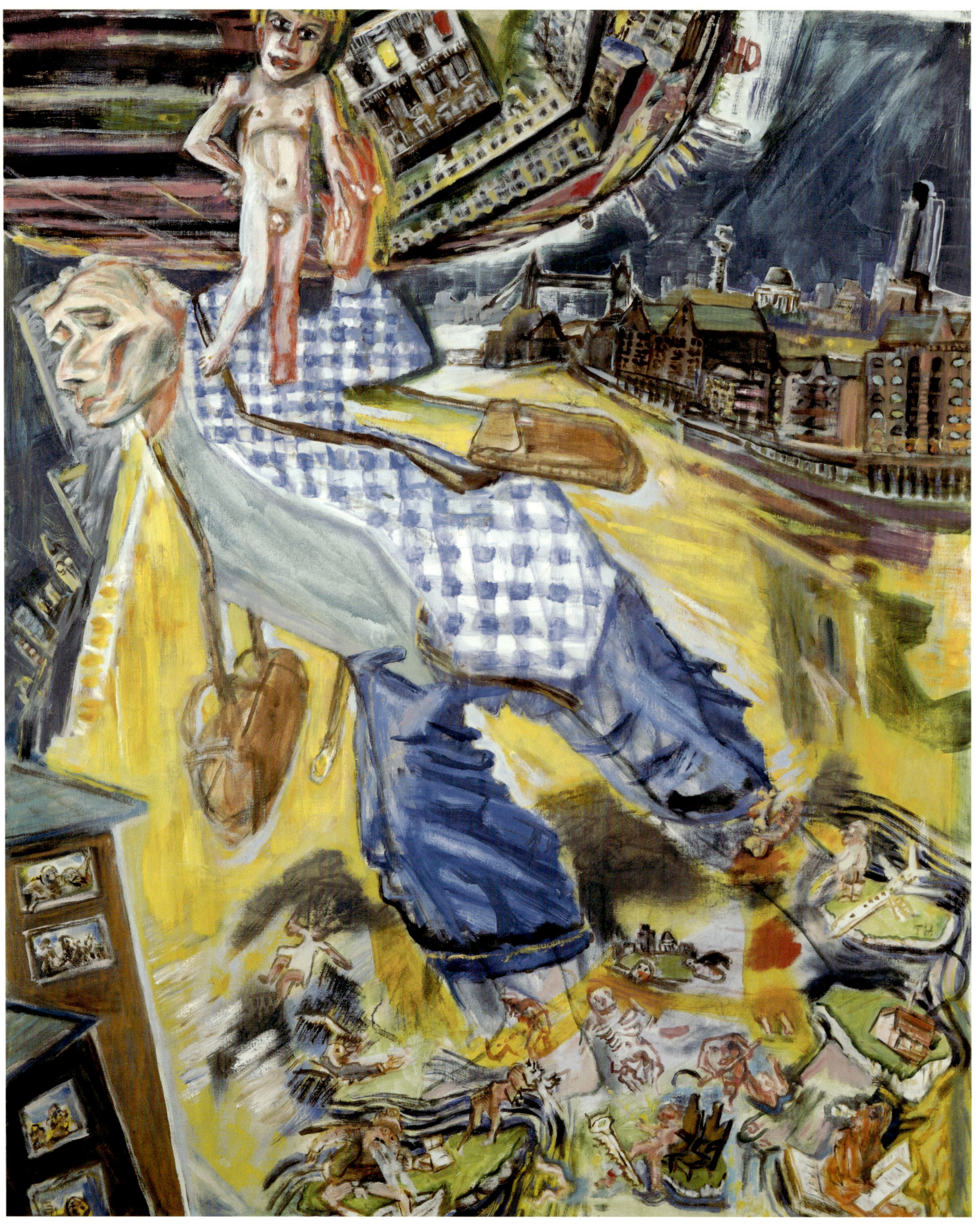

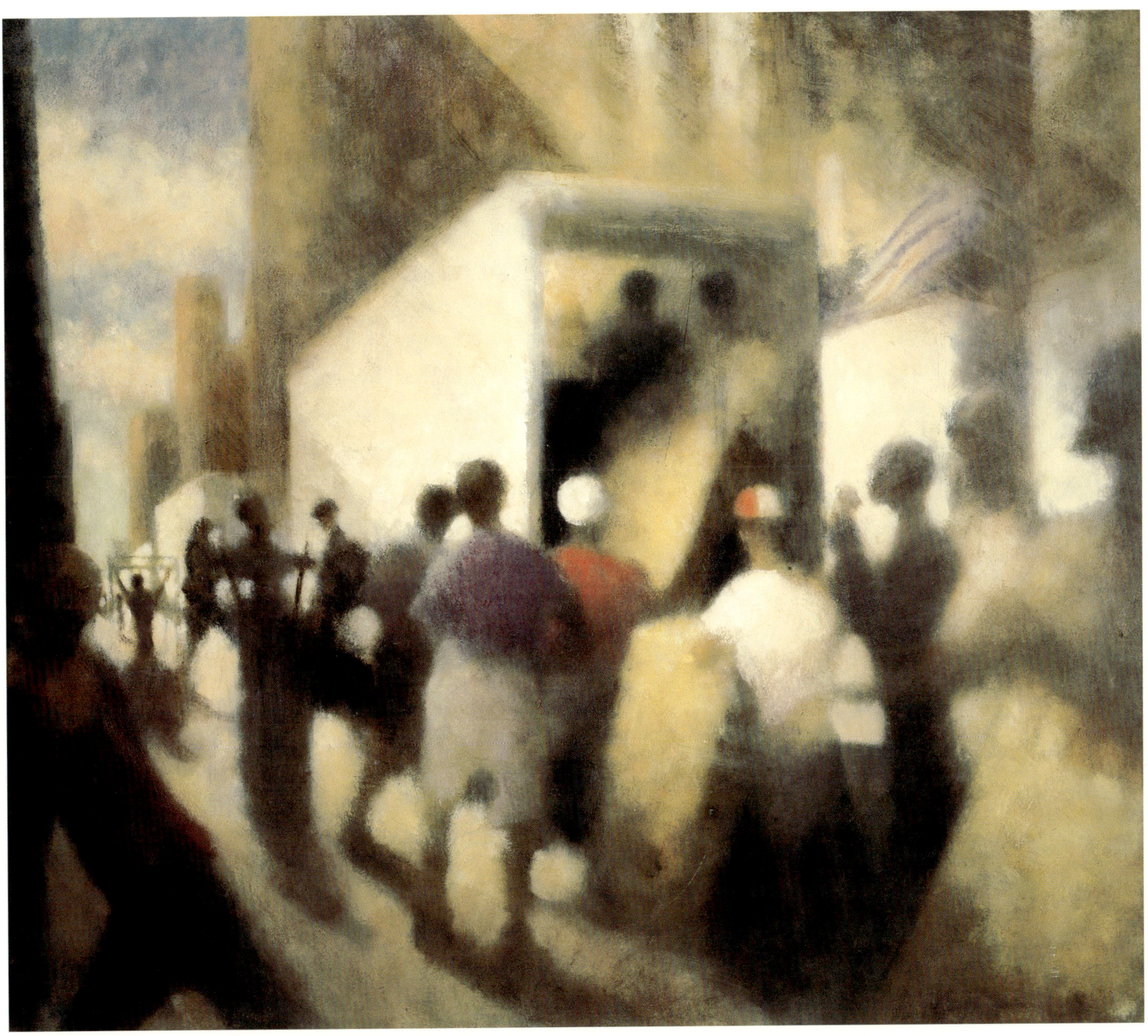

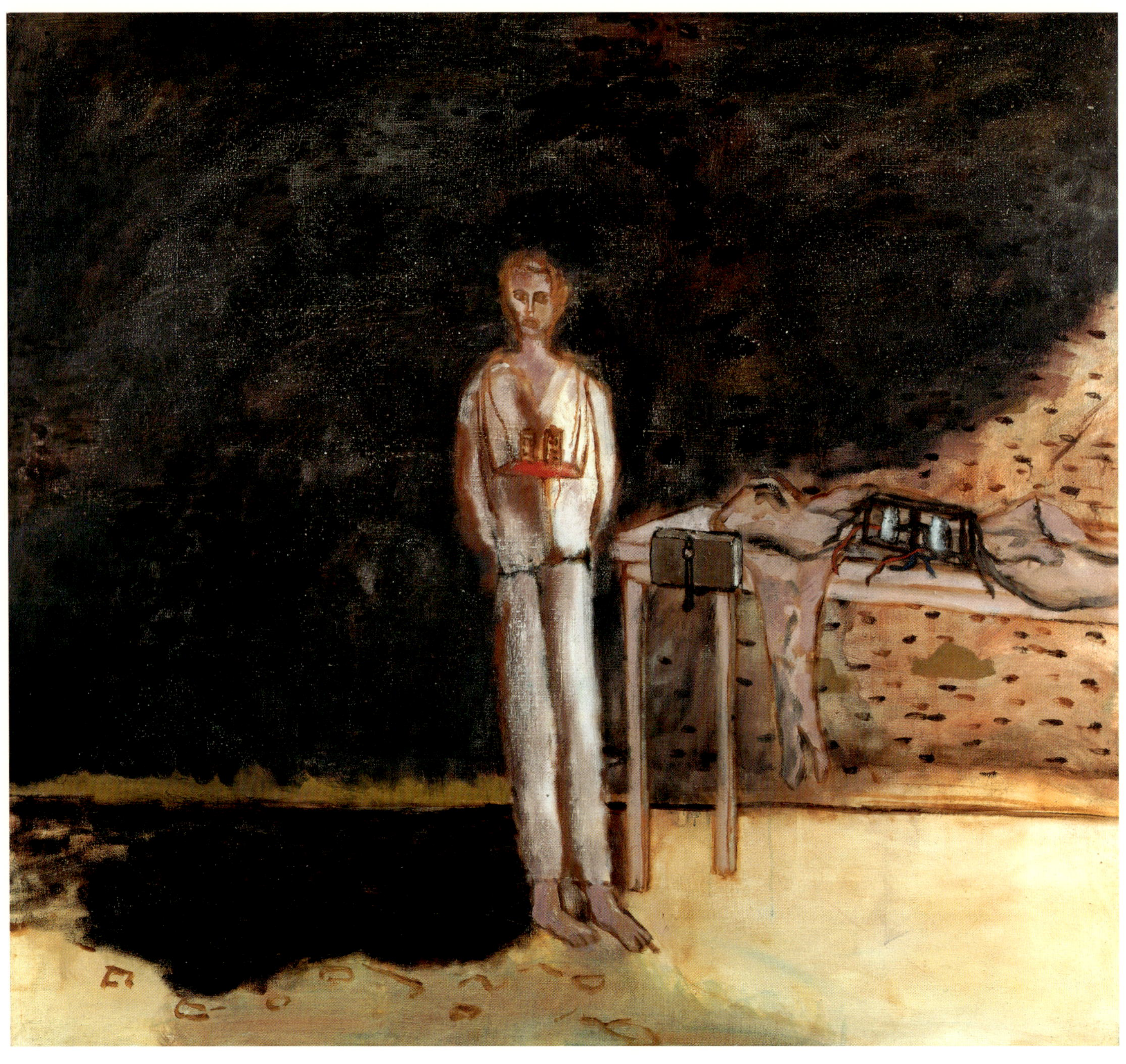

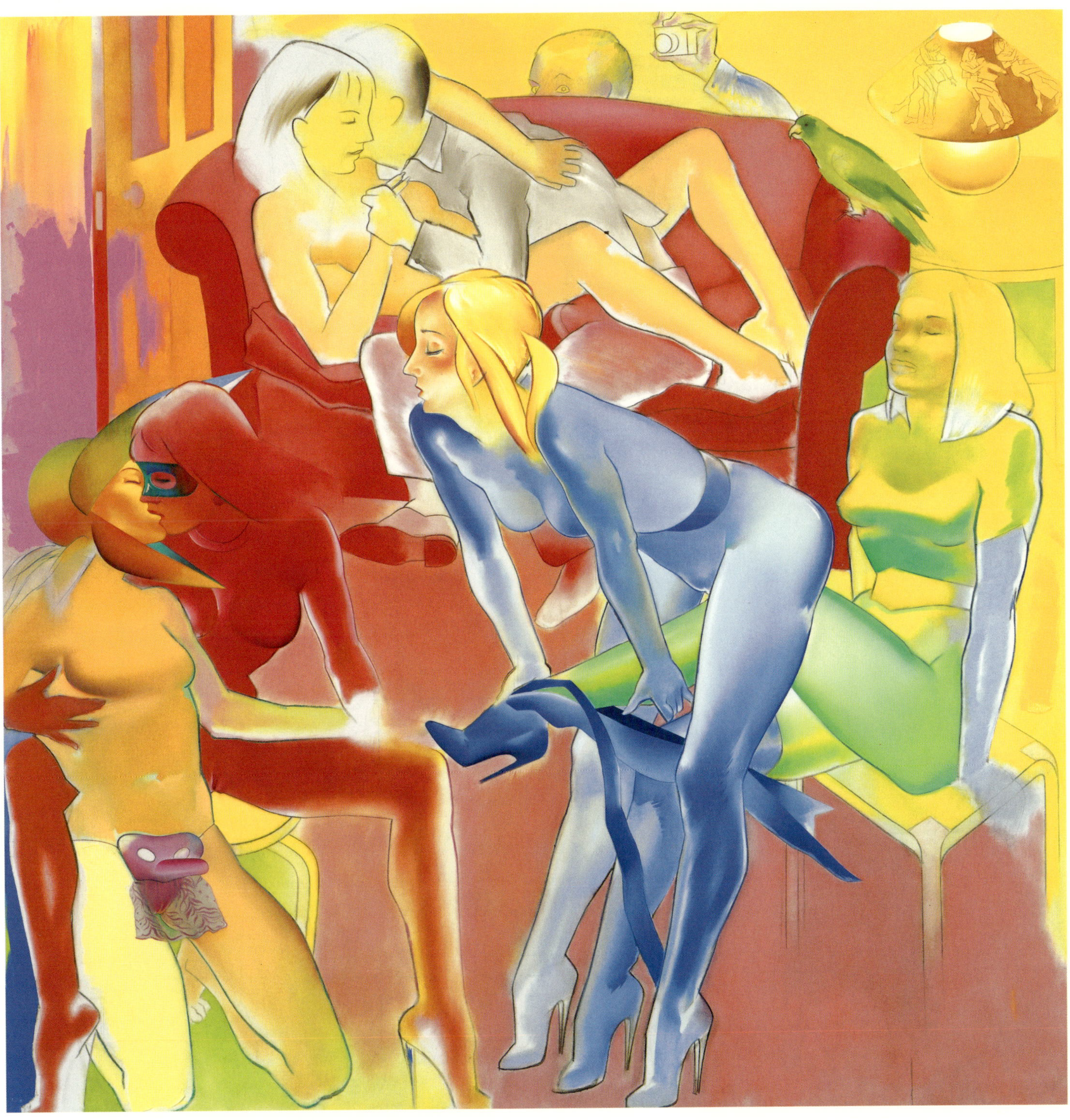

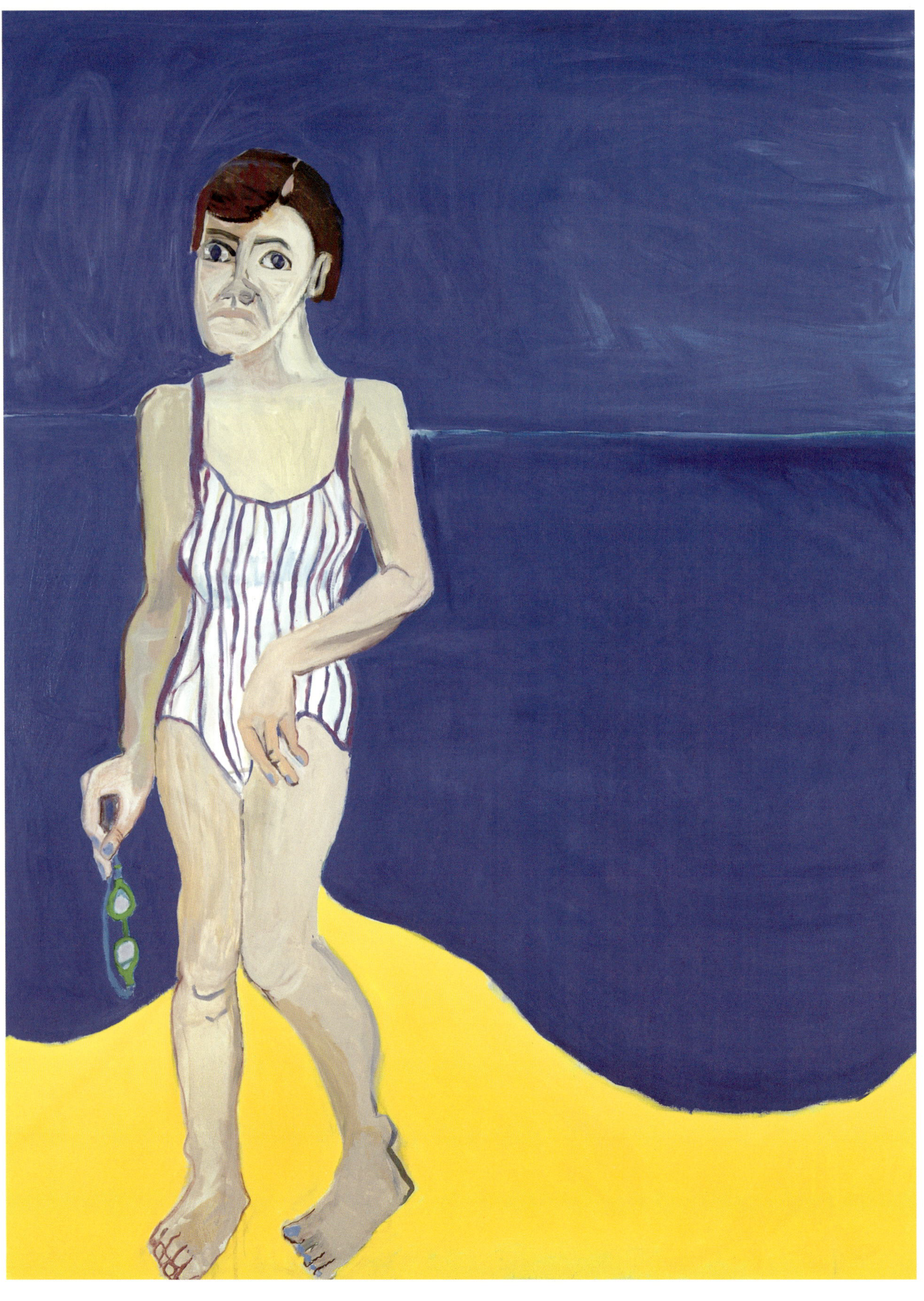

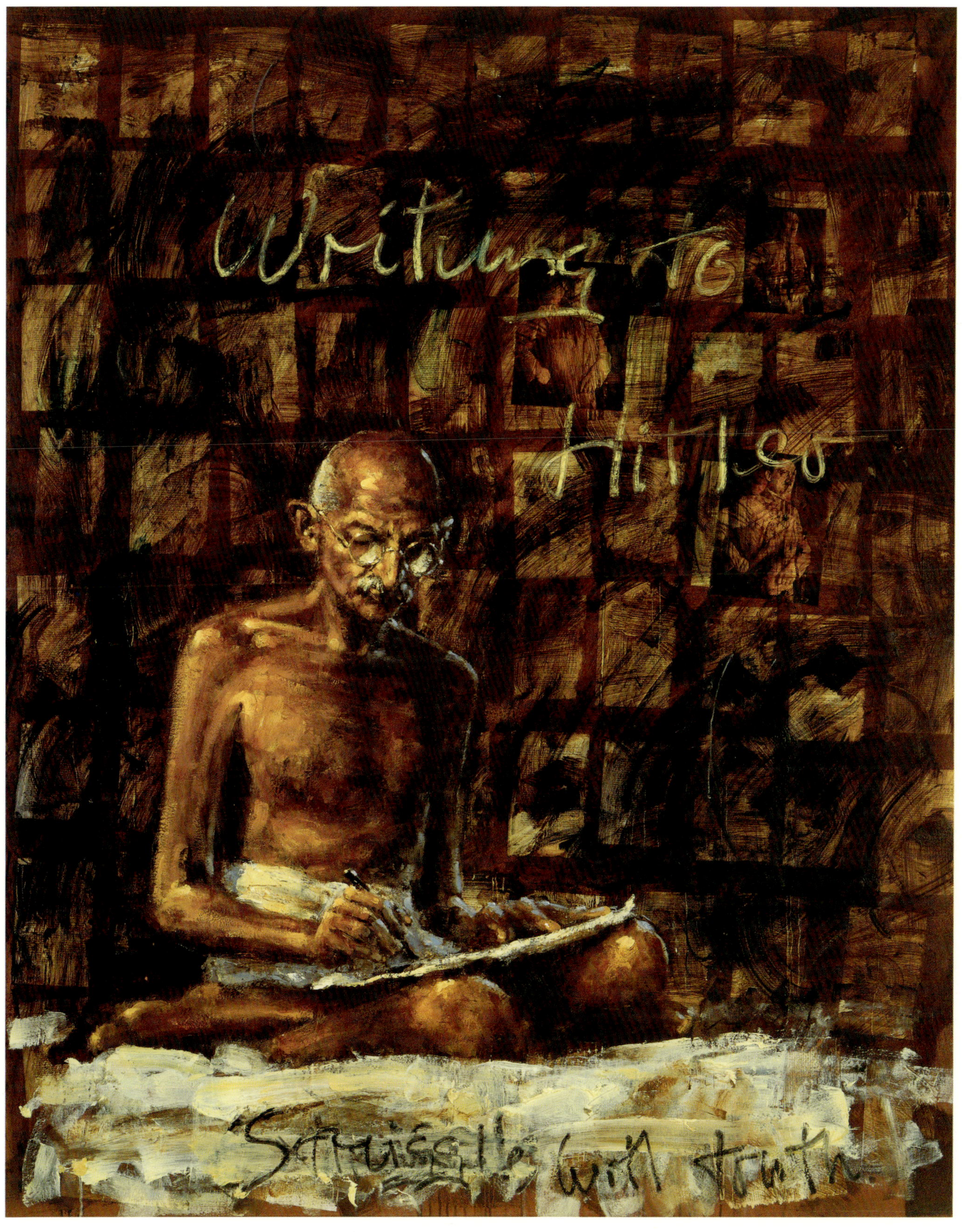
Writing to
Hitler
Struggle with truth

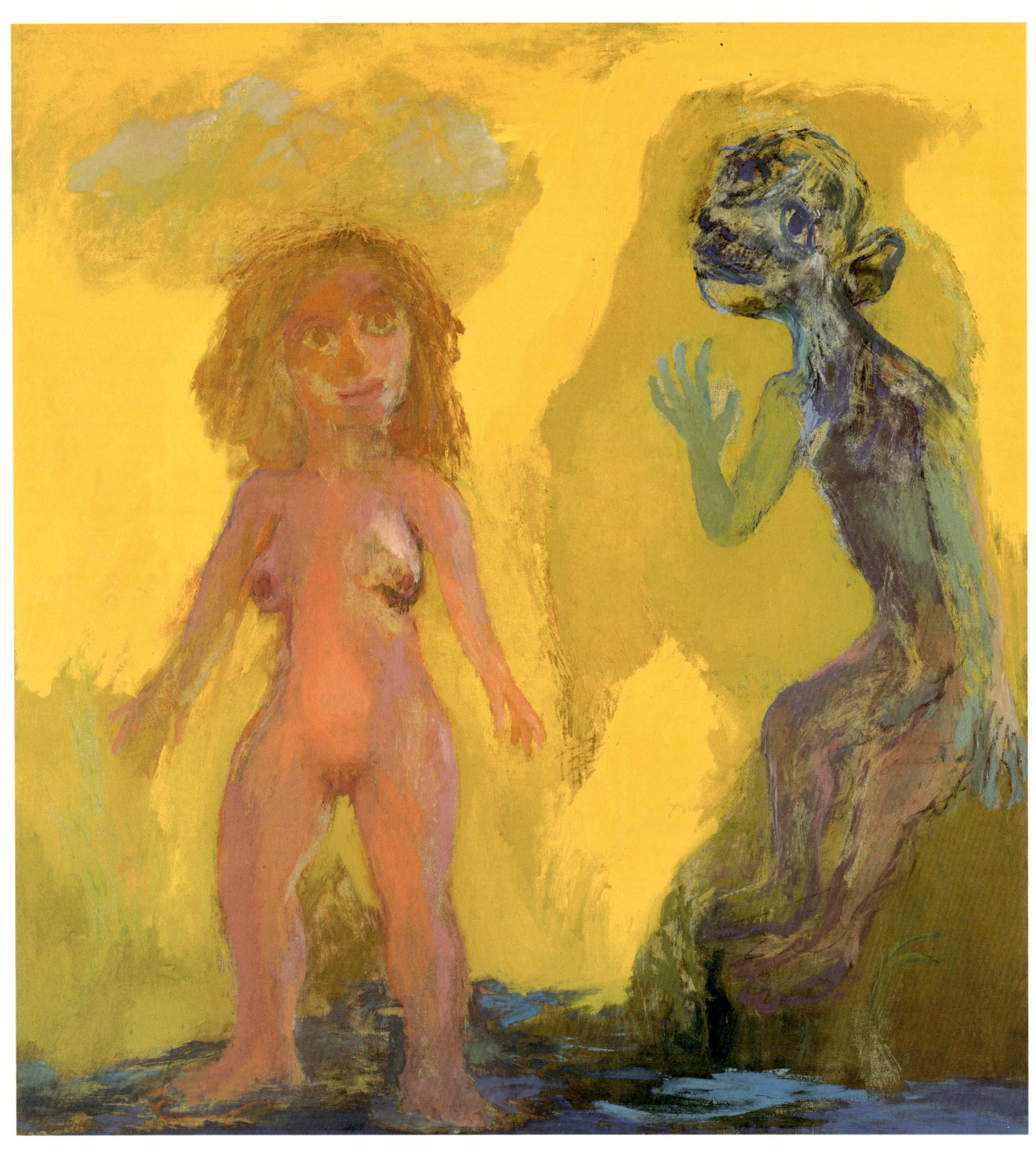

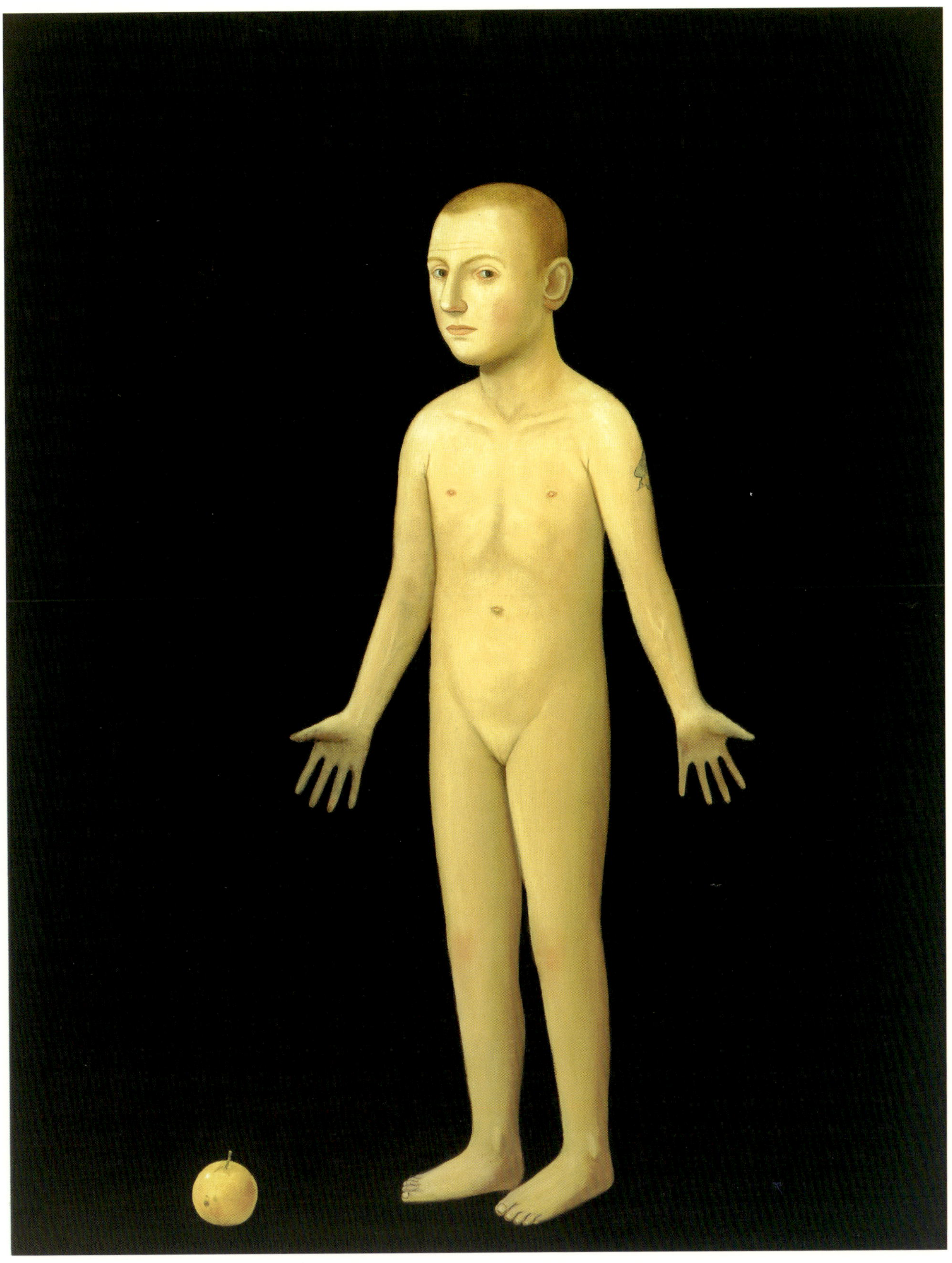

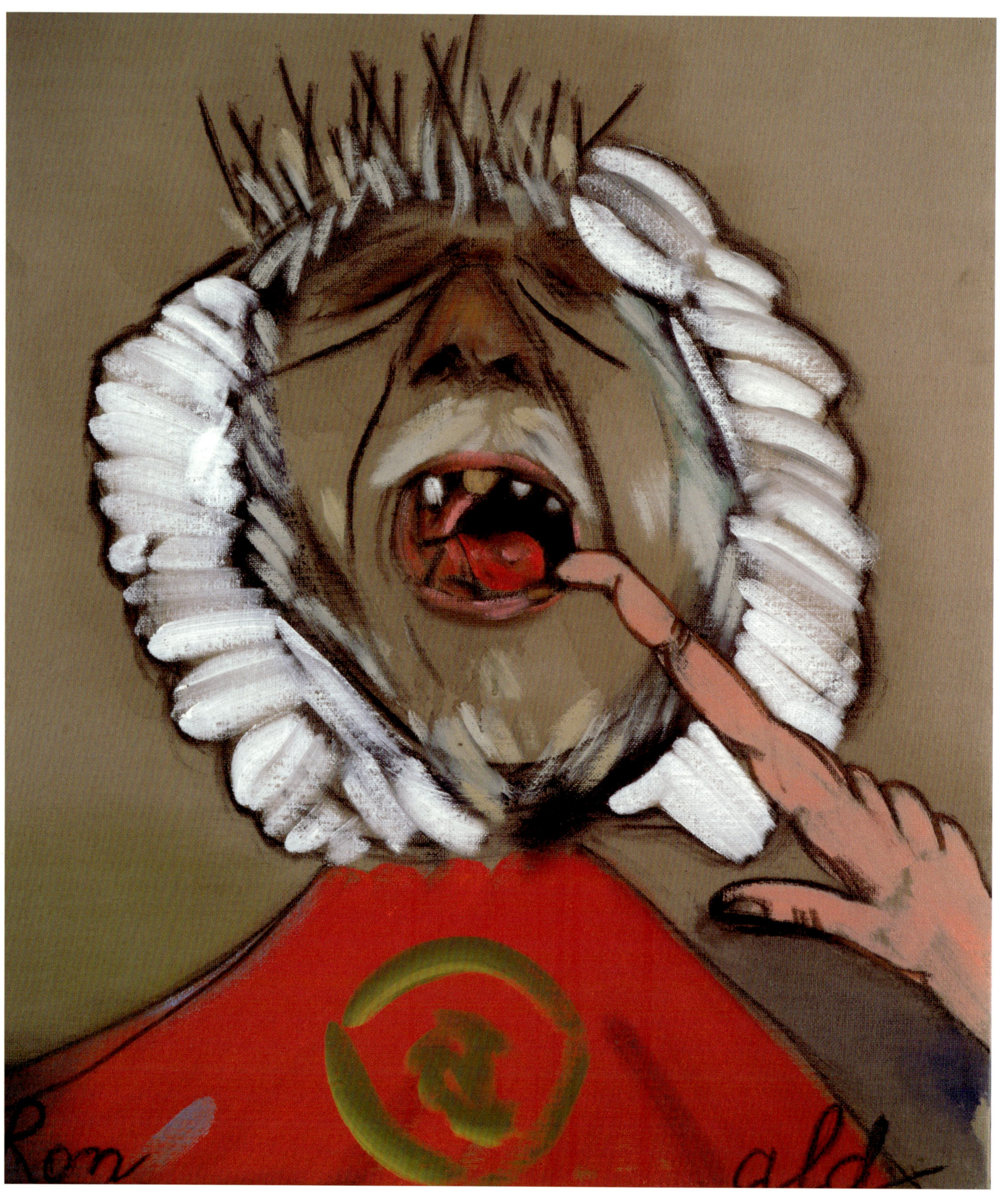
Ron
ald

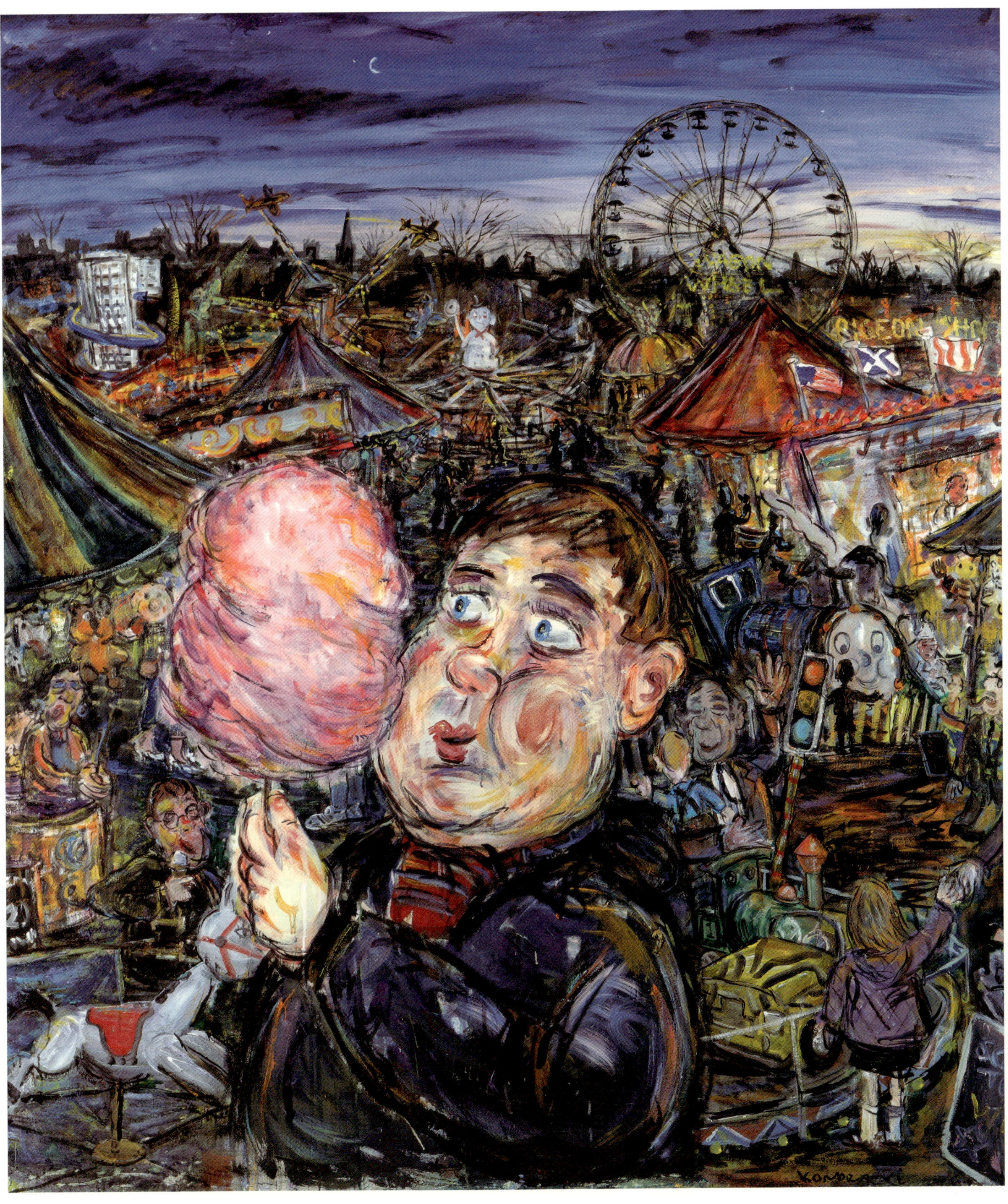

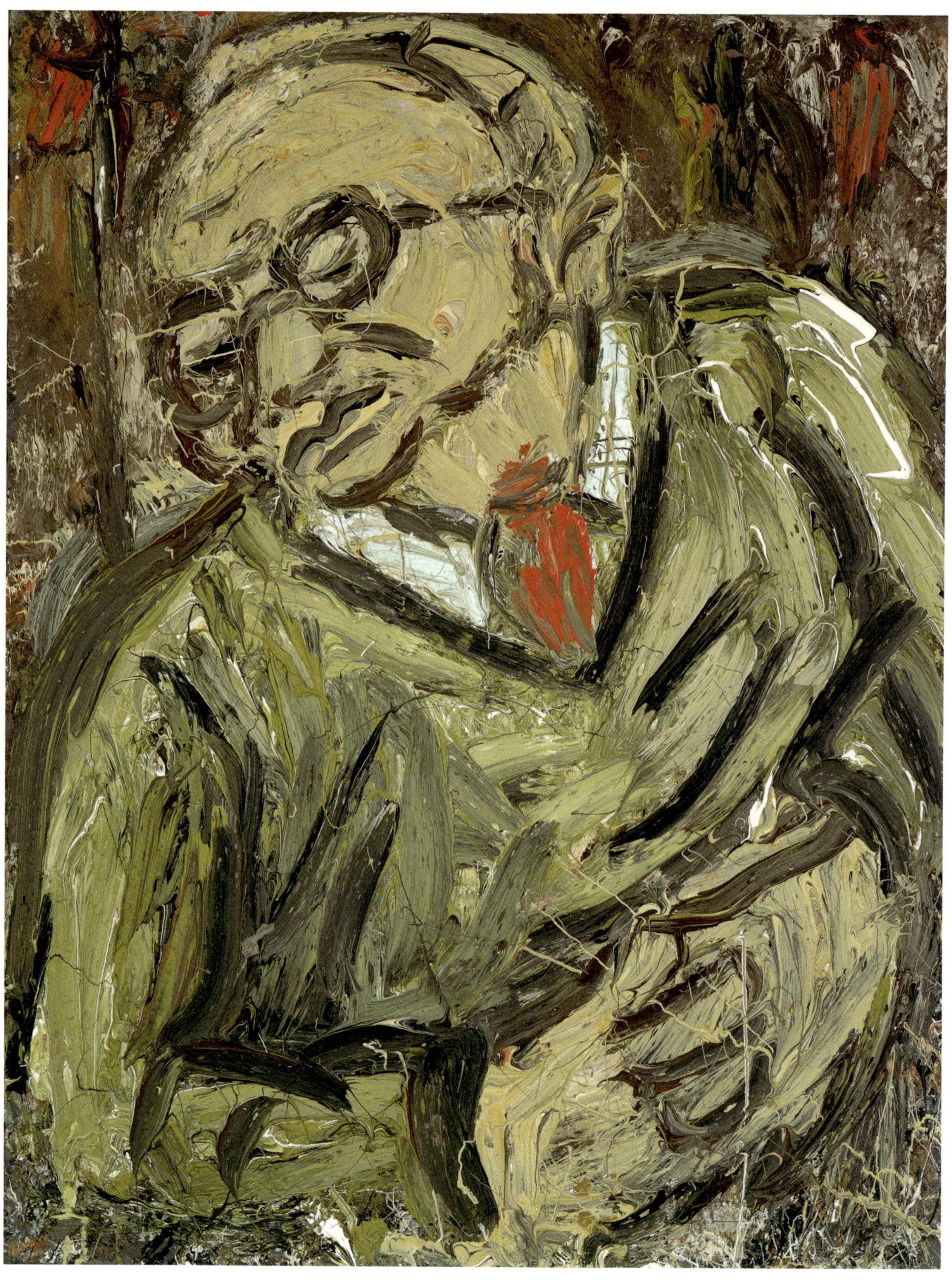

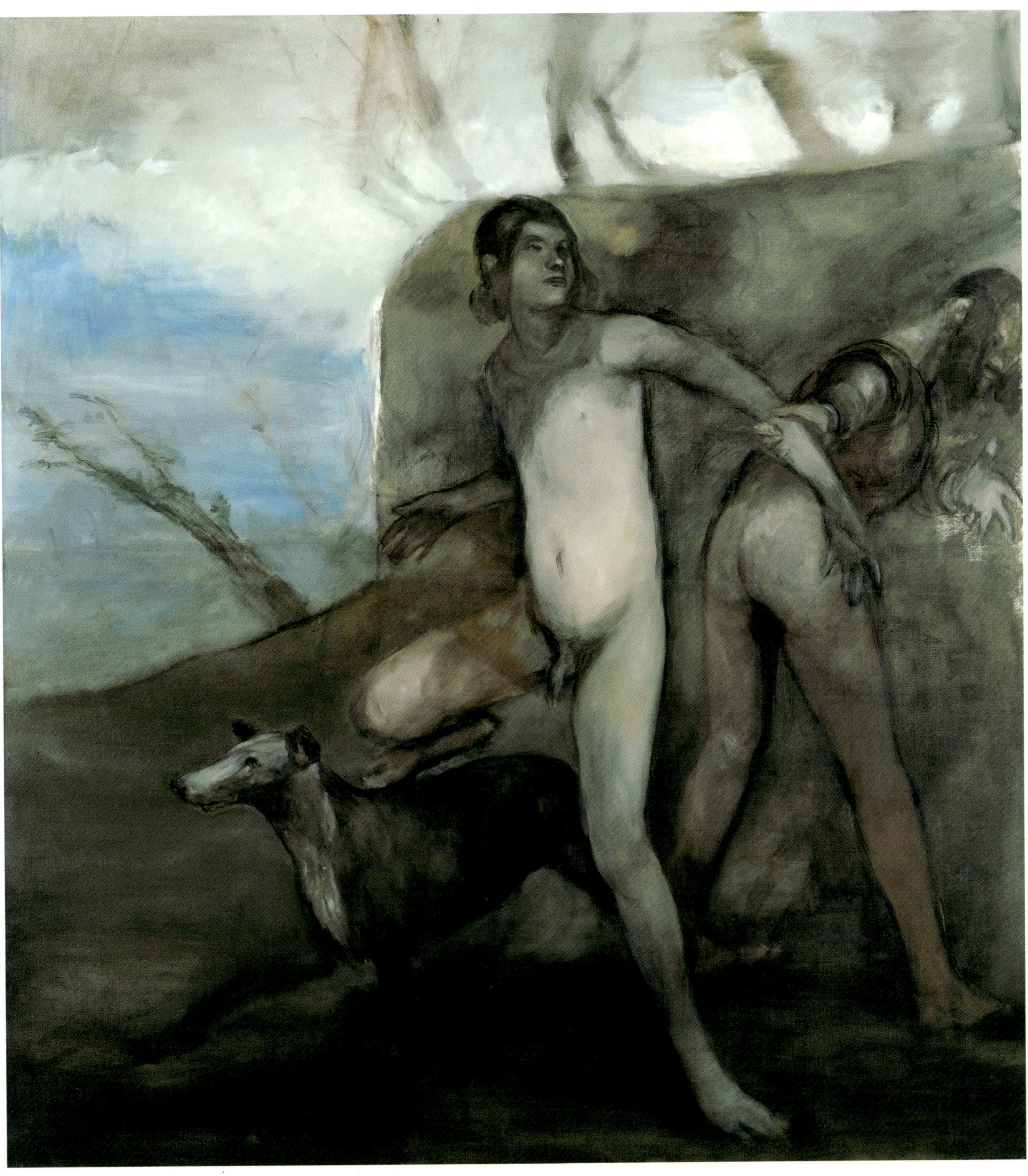

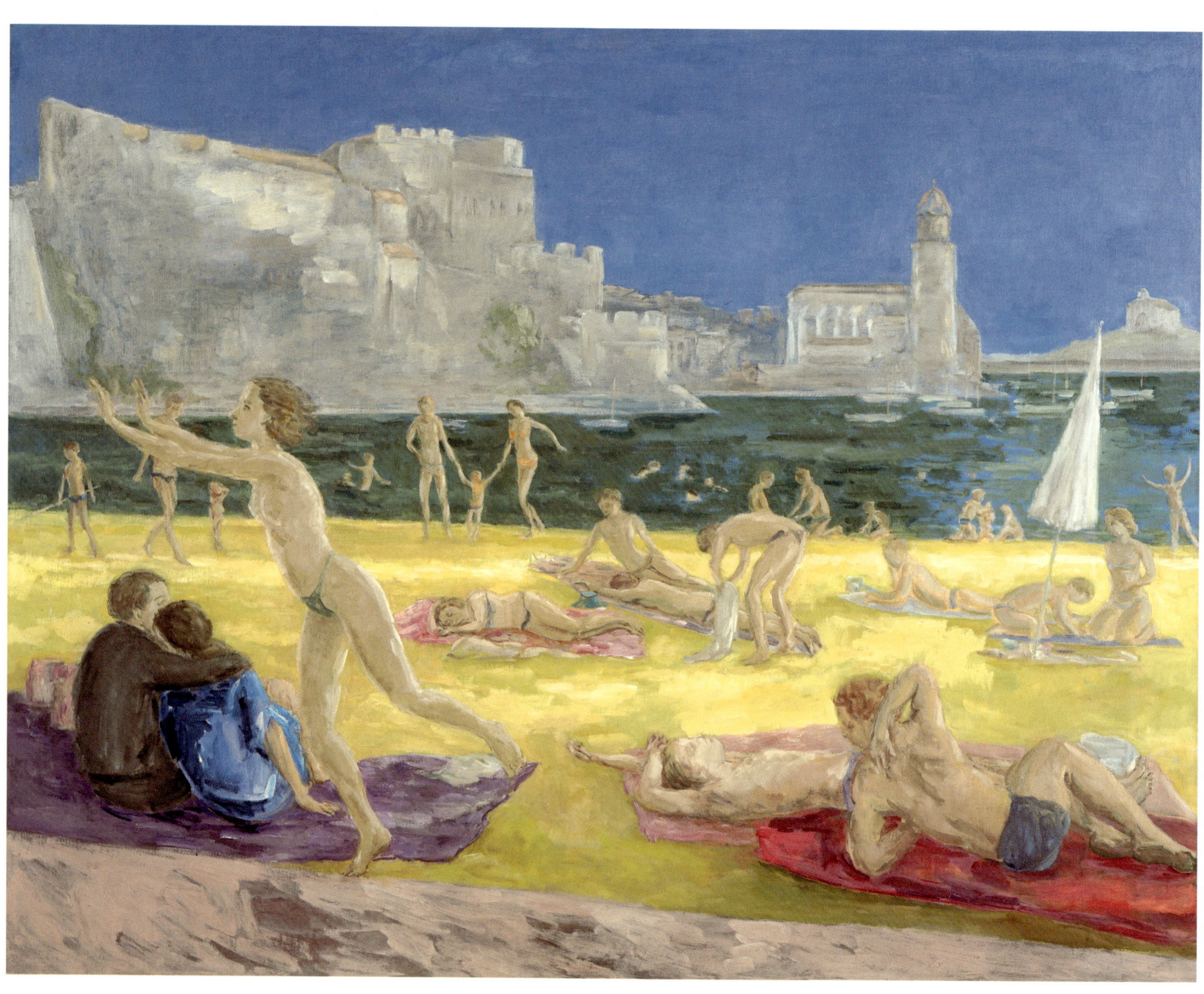

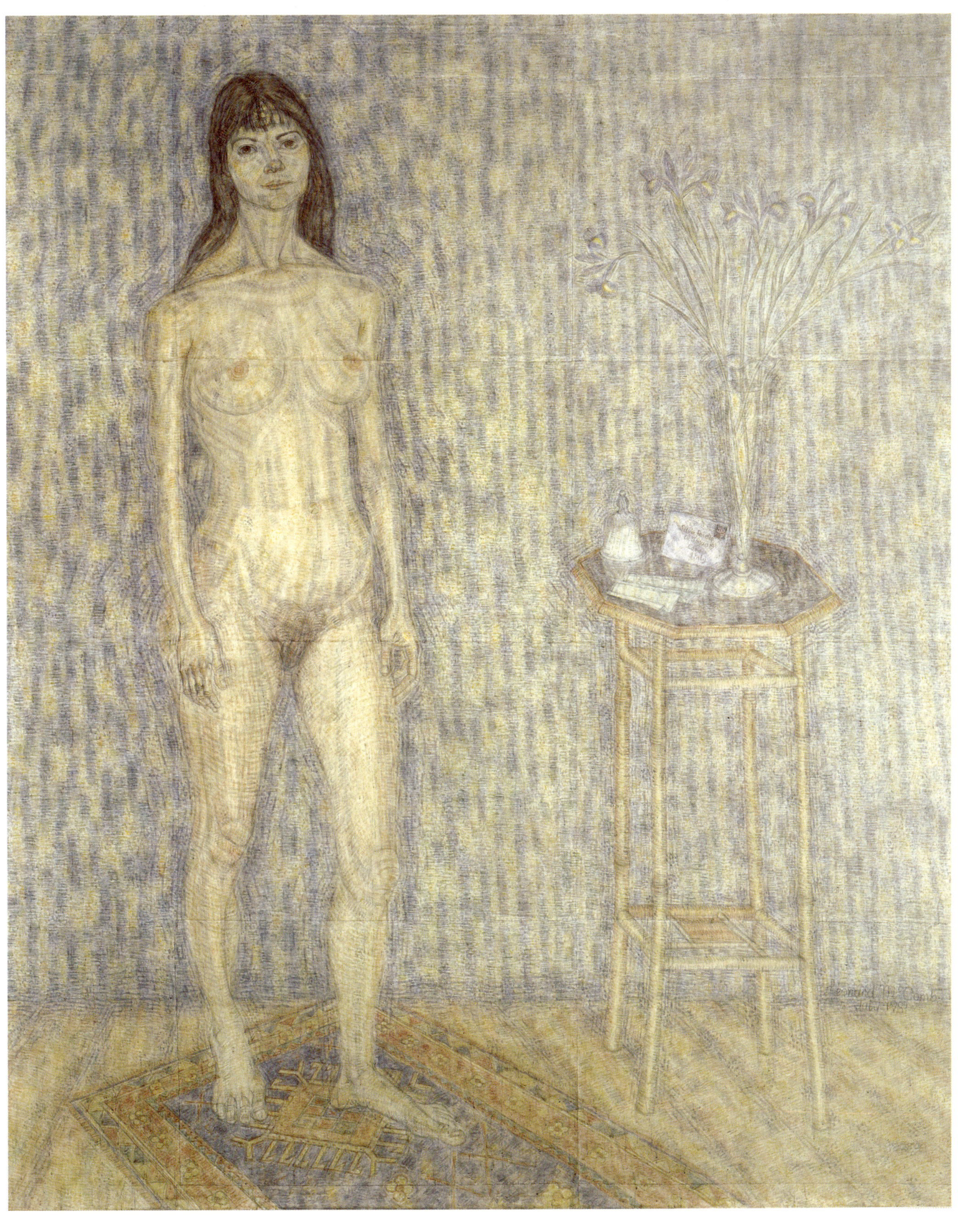

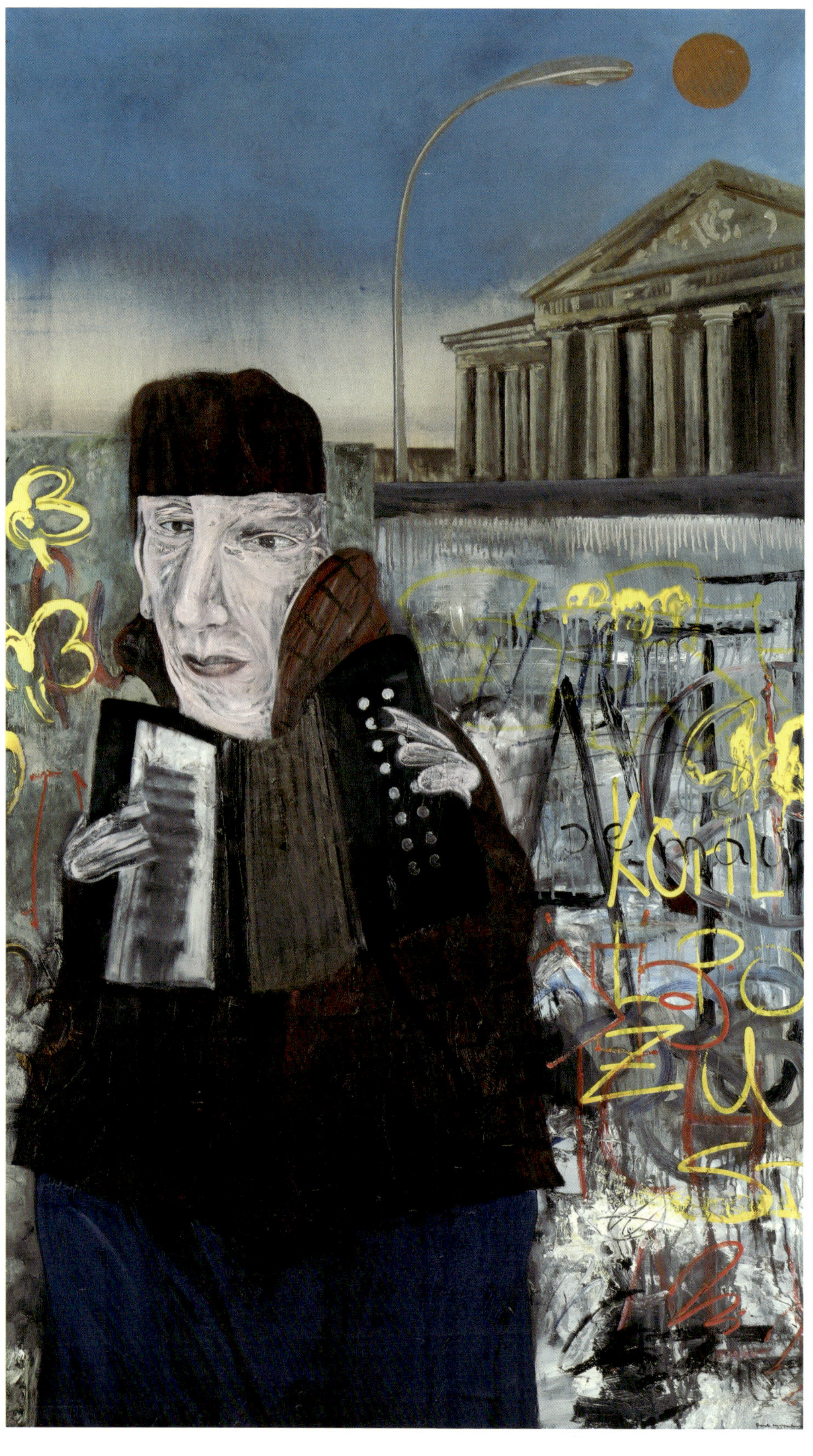

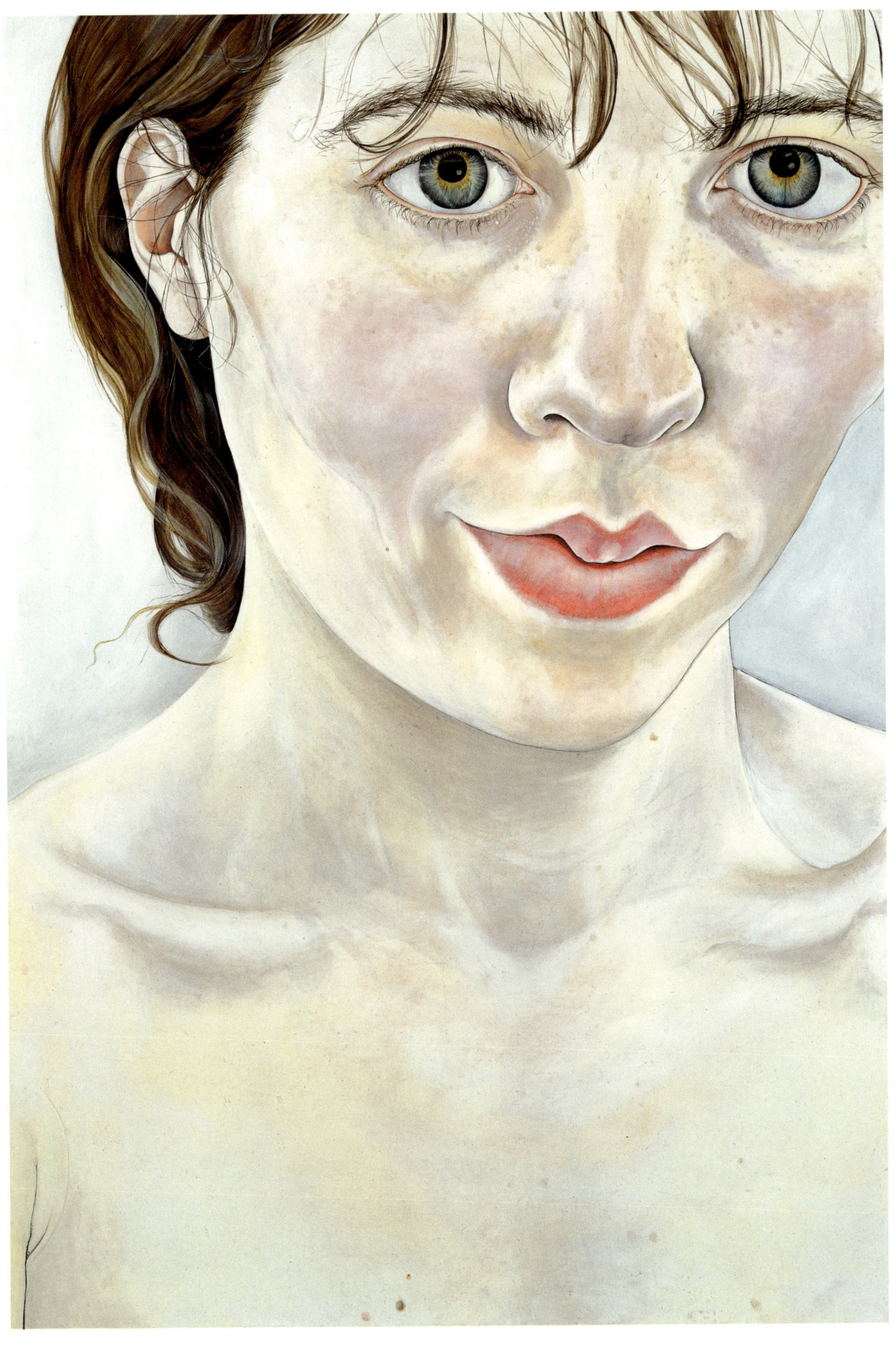

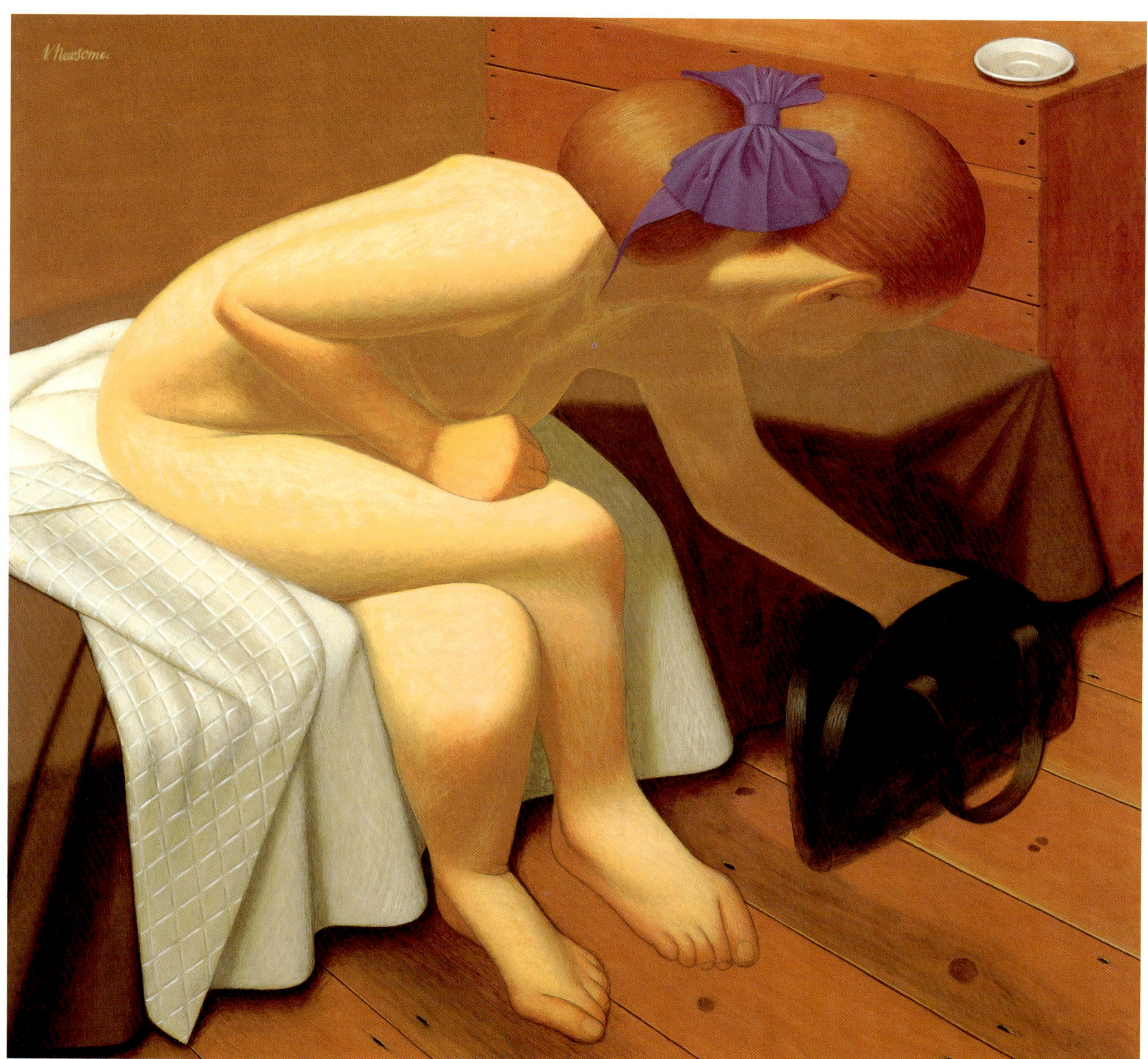
V Newsome

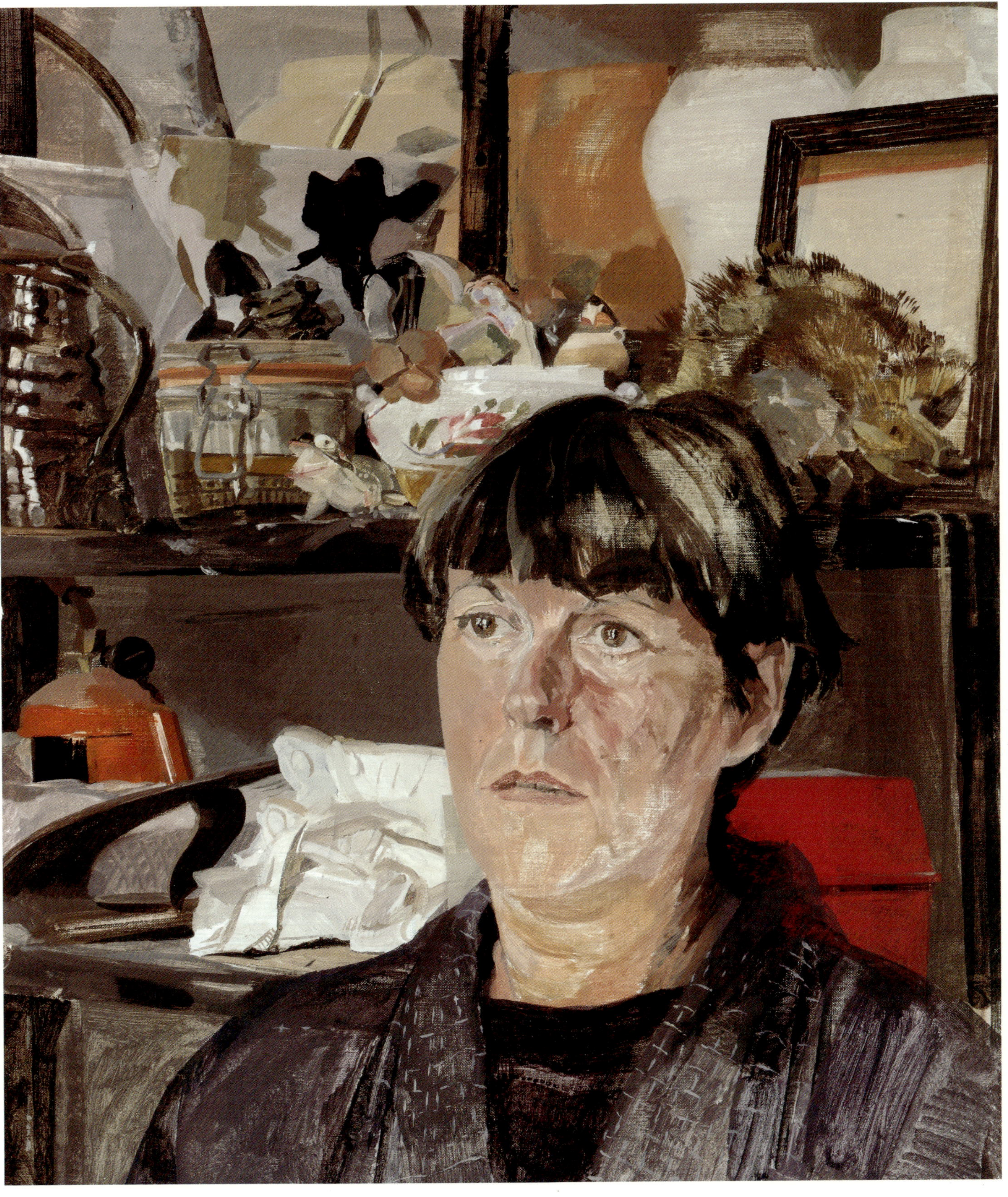

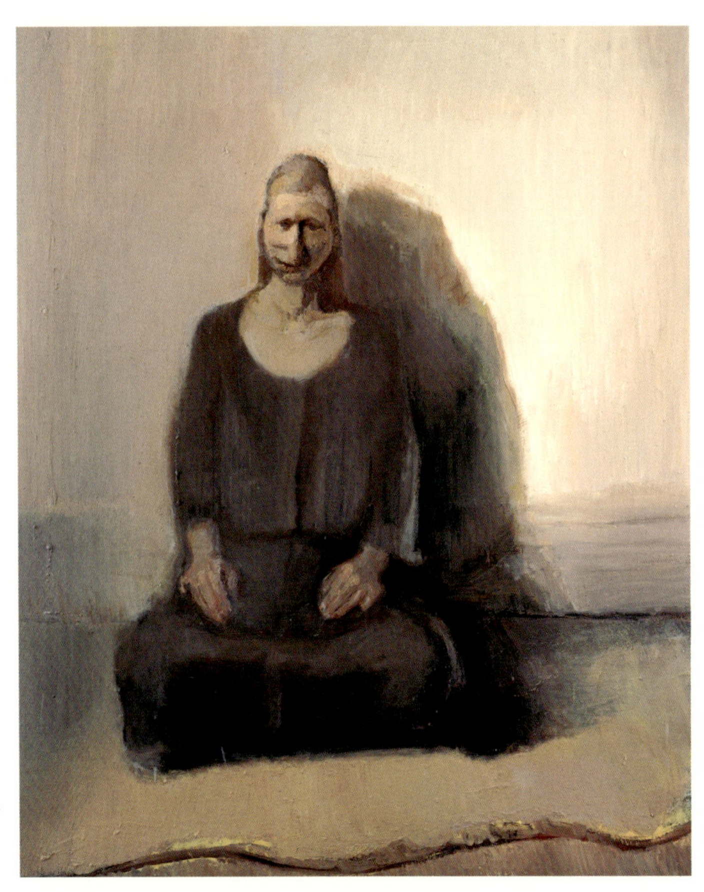

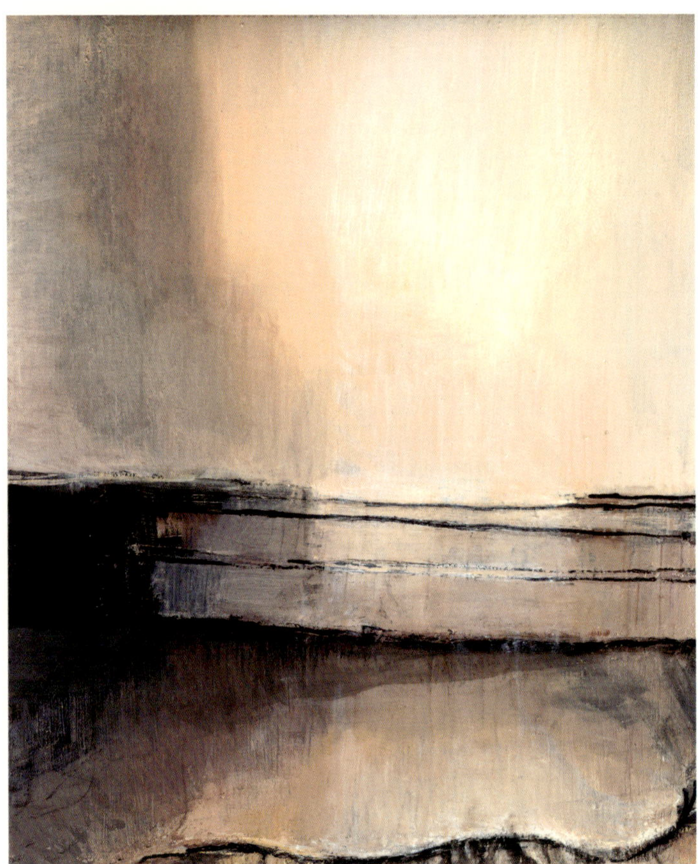

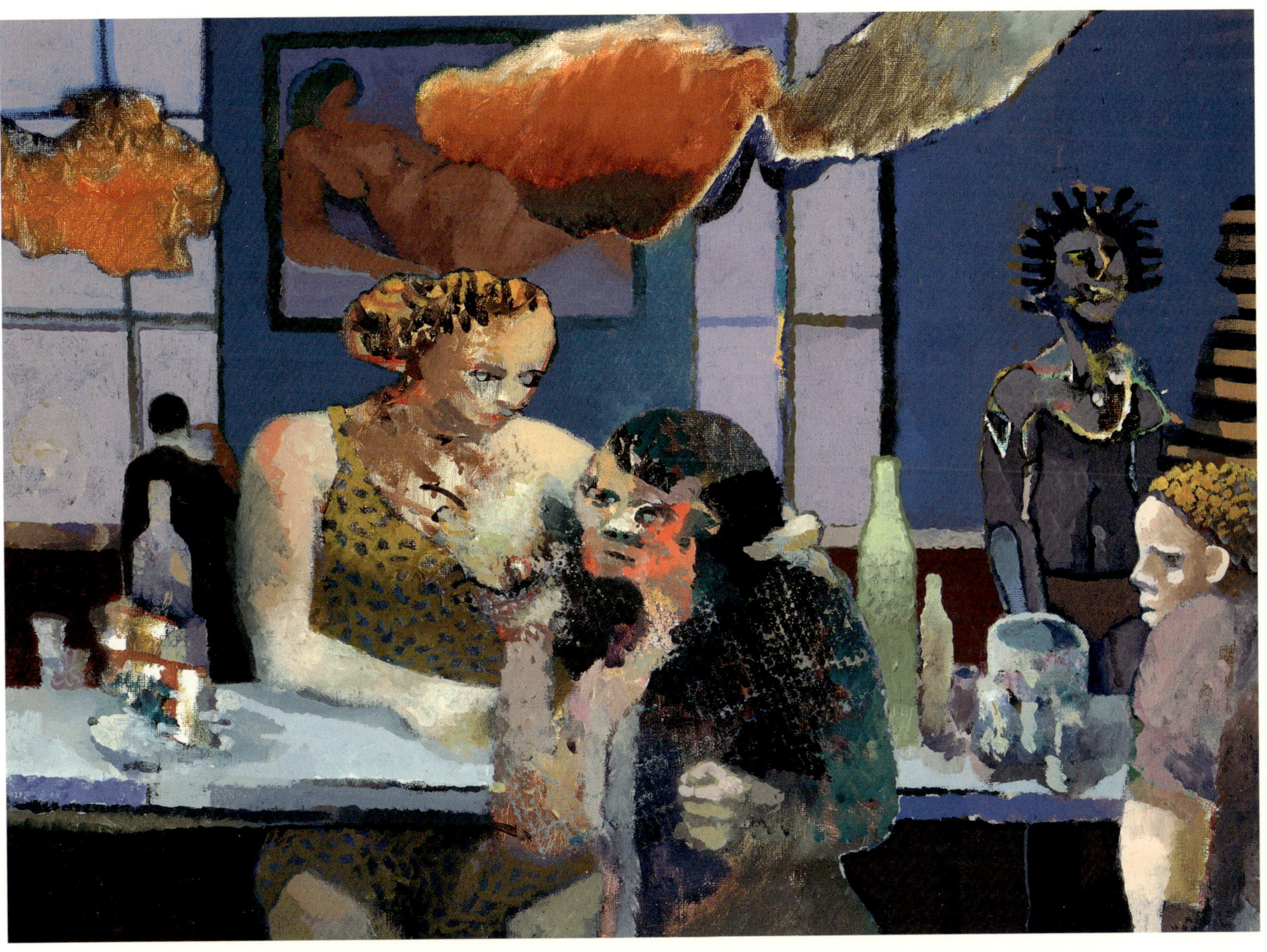

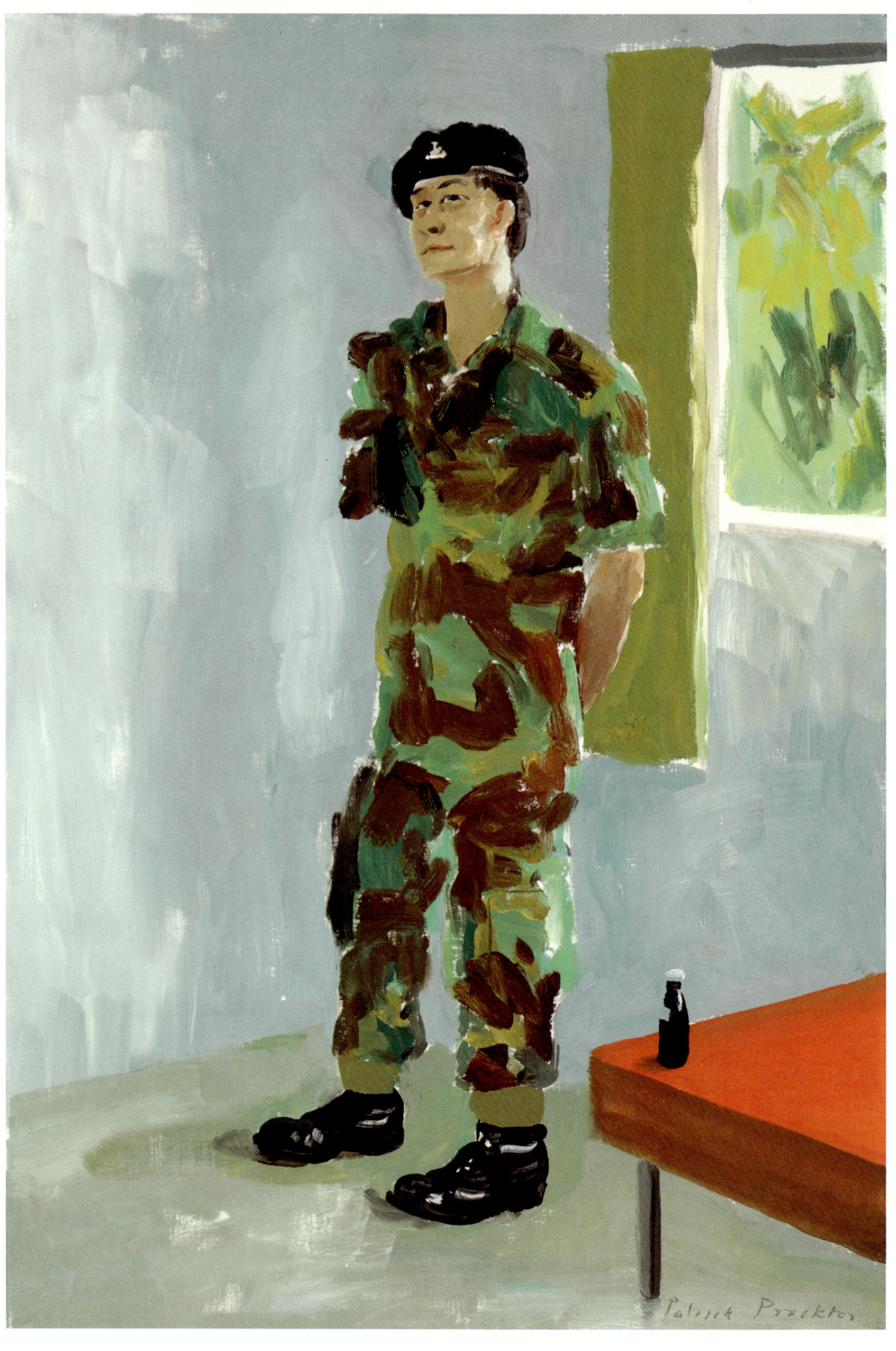
Patrick Procktor

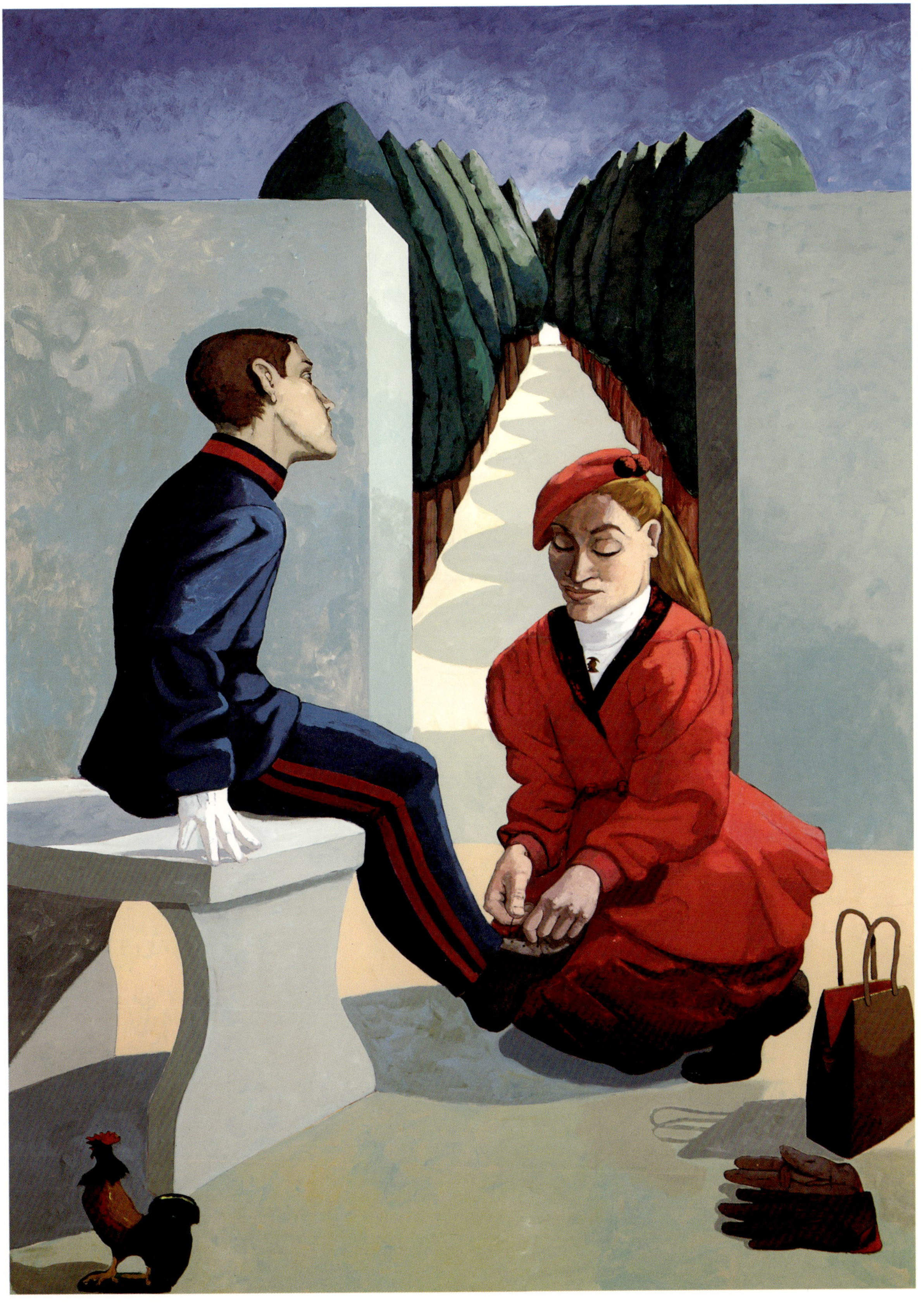

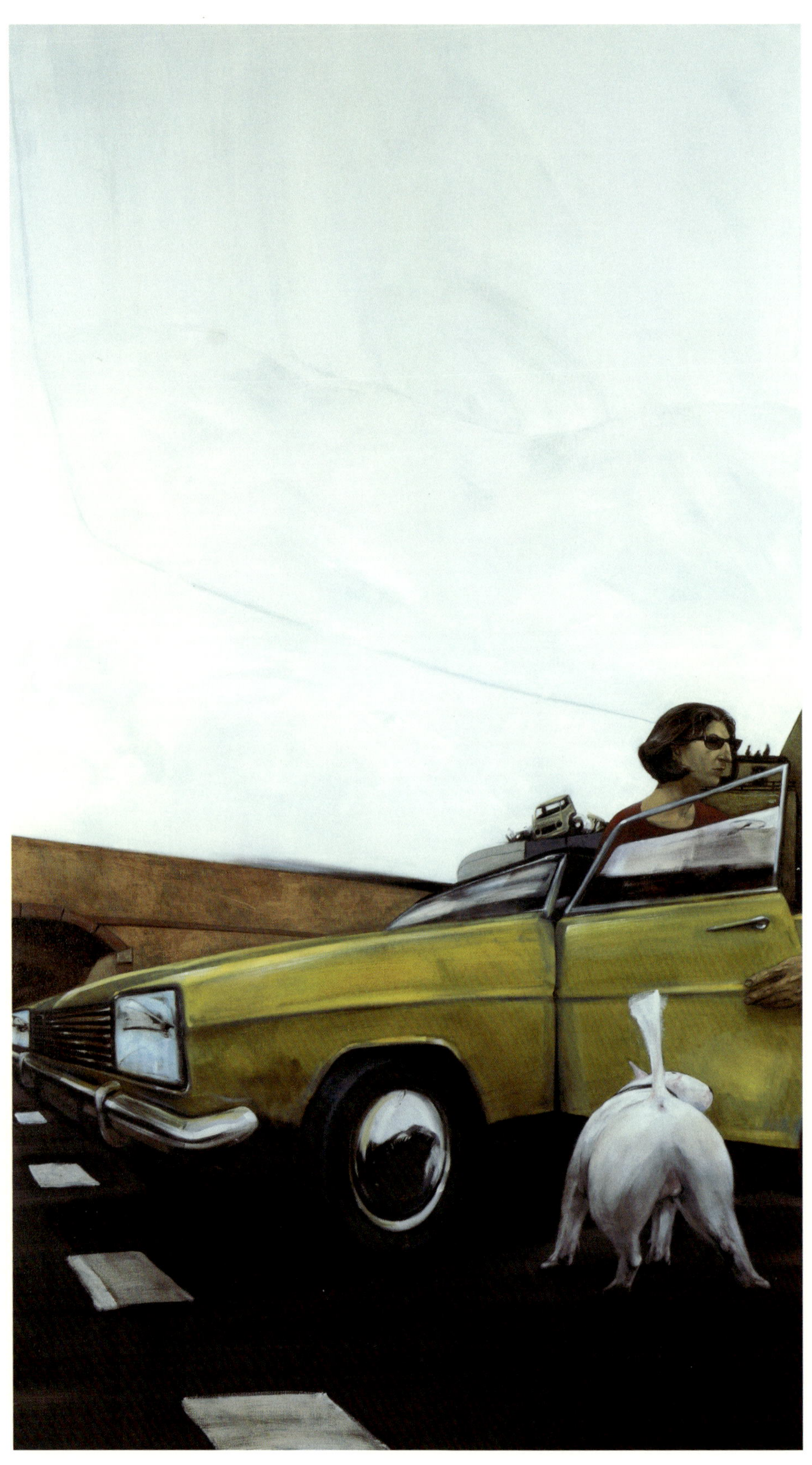

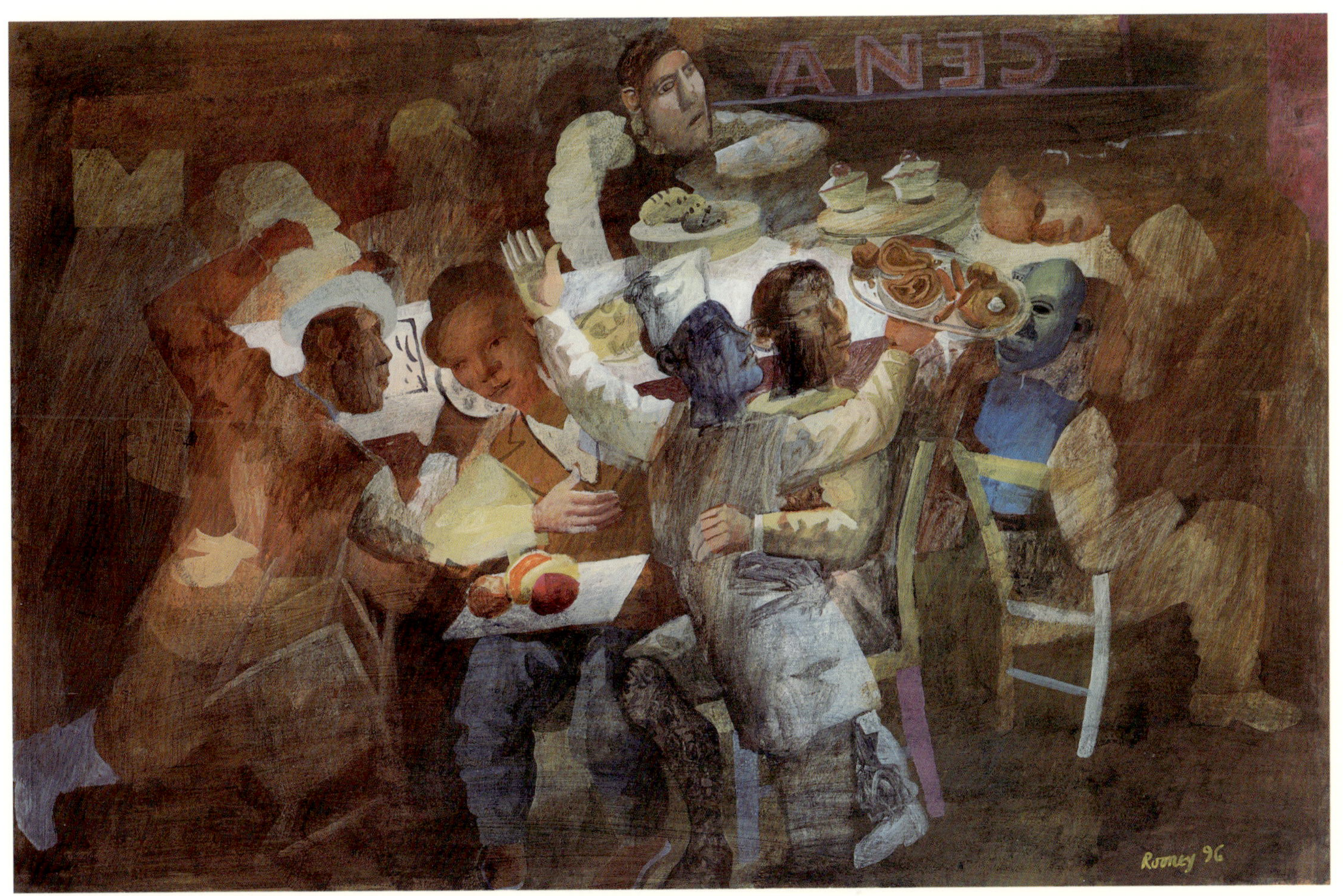
Rooney 96

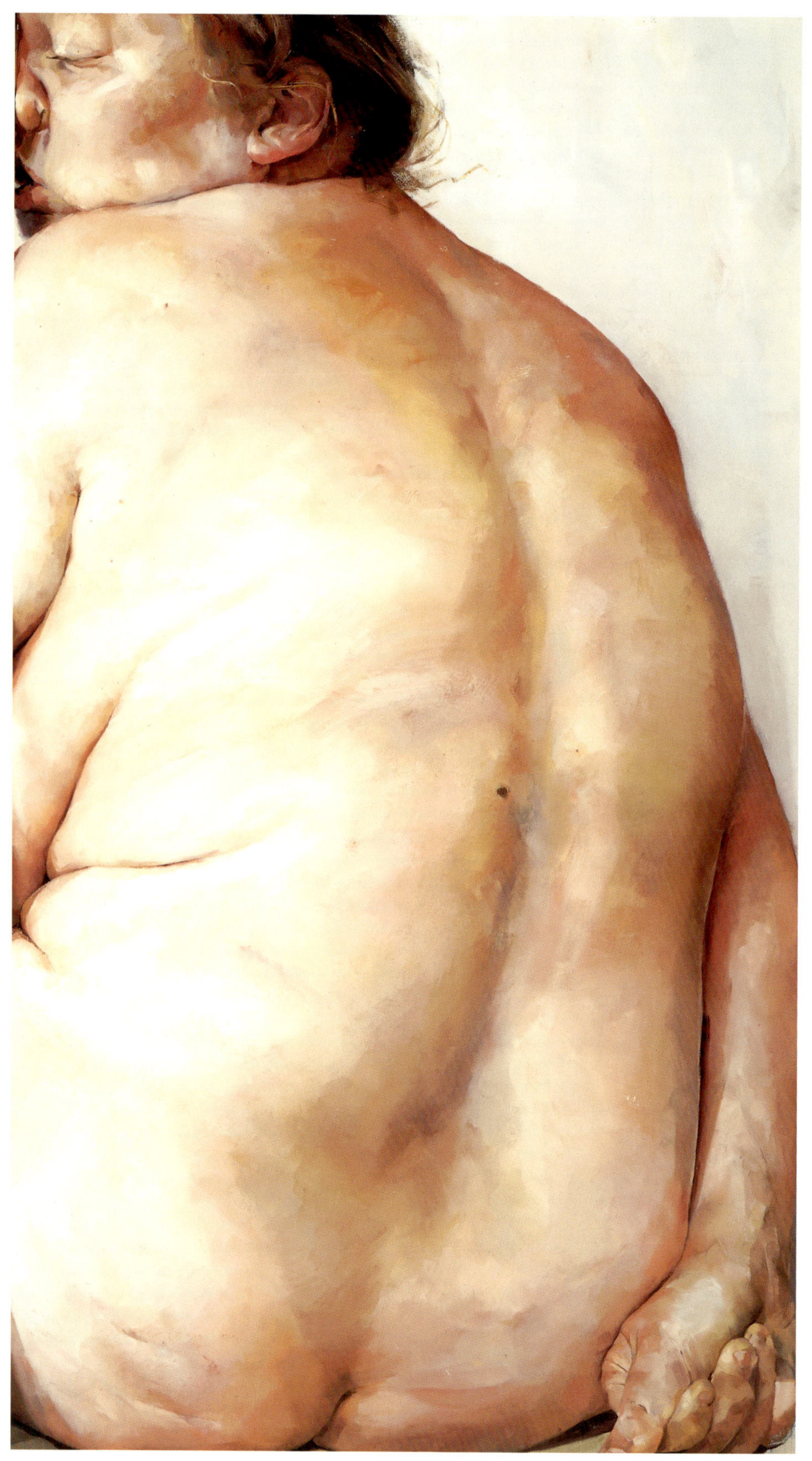

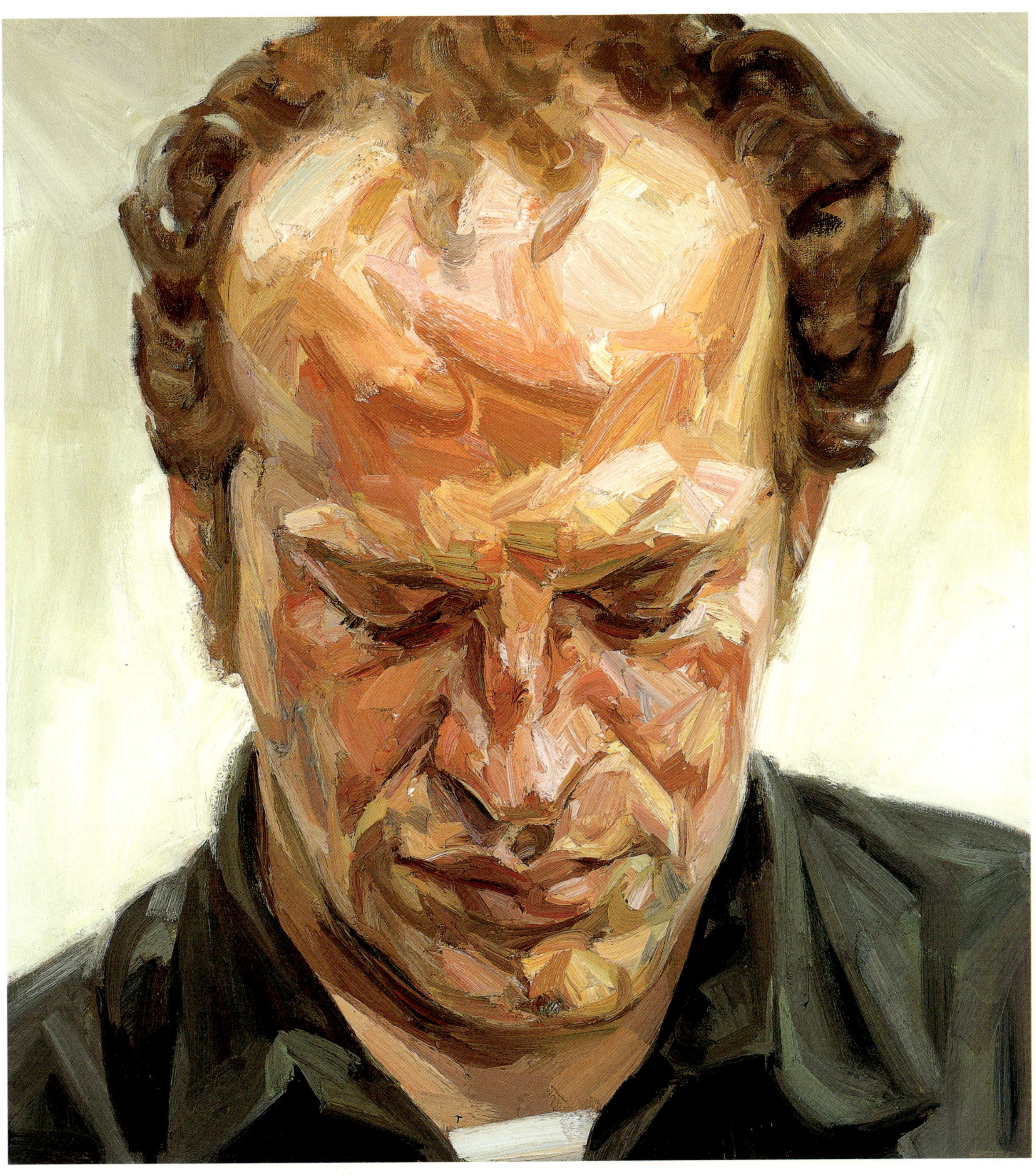

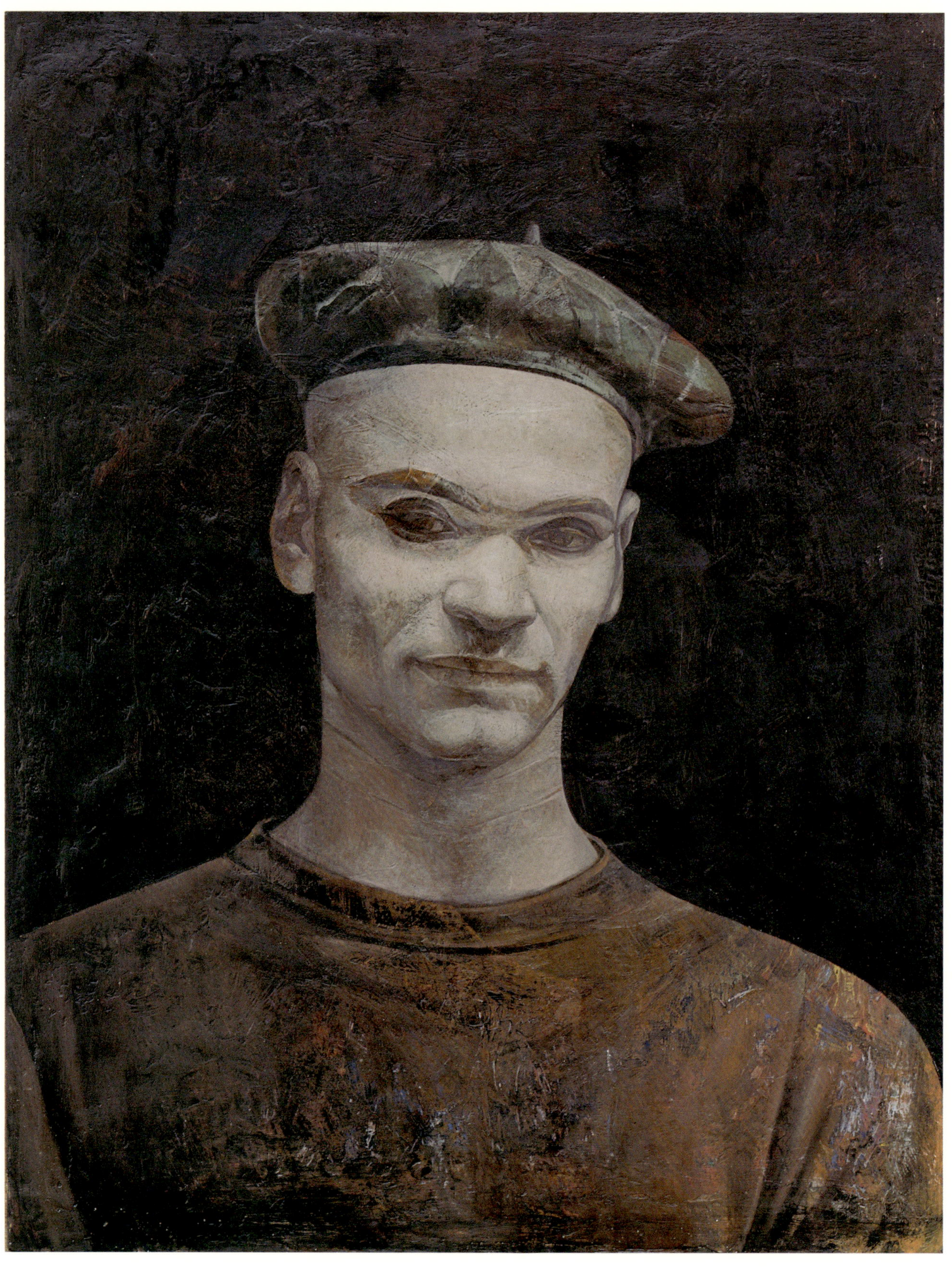

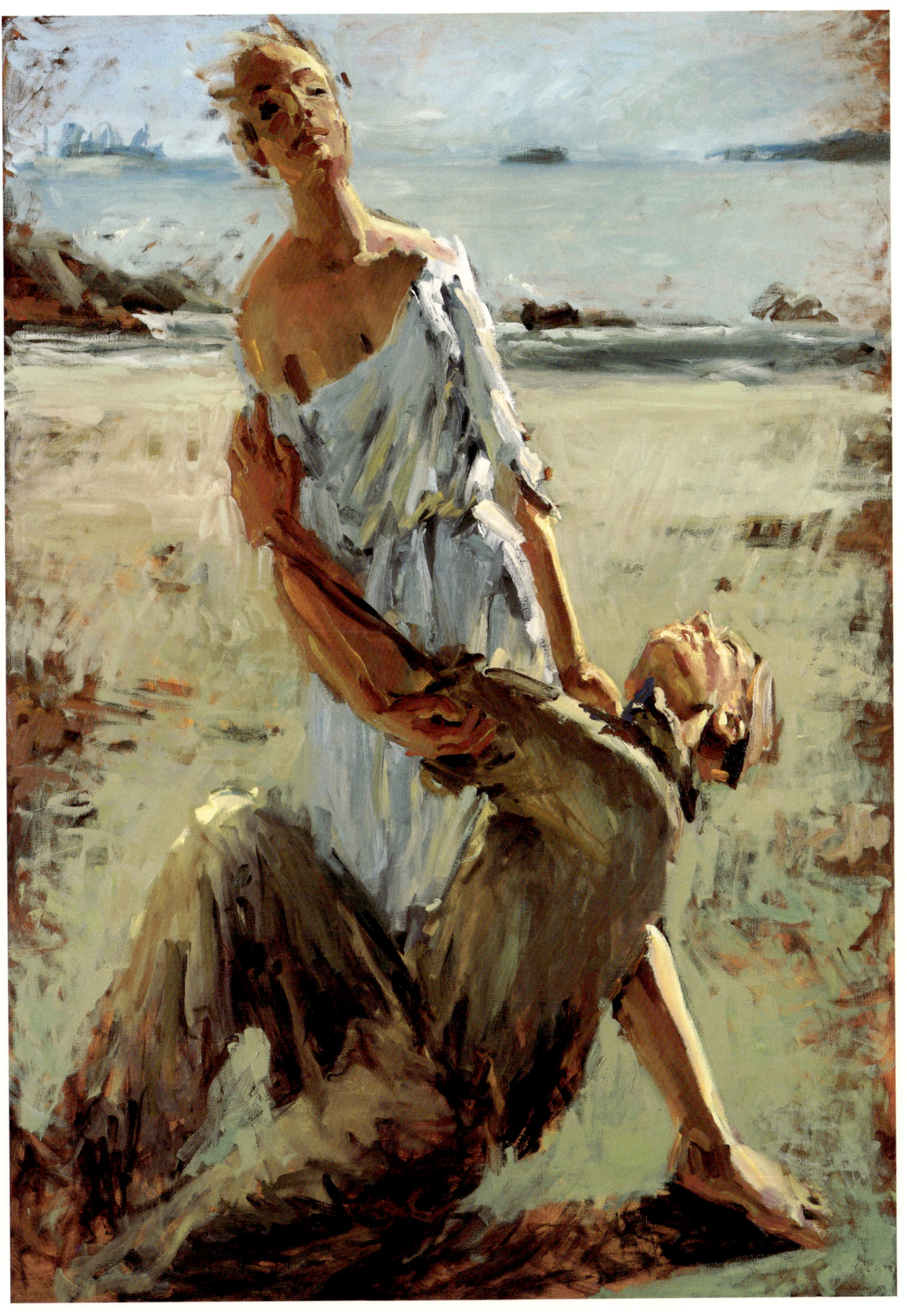

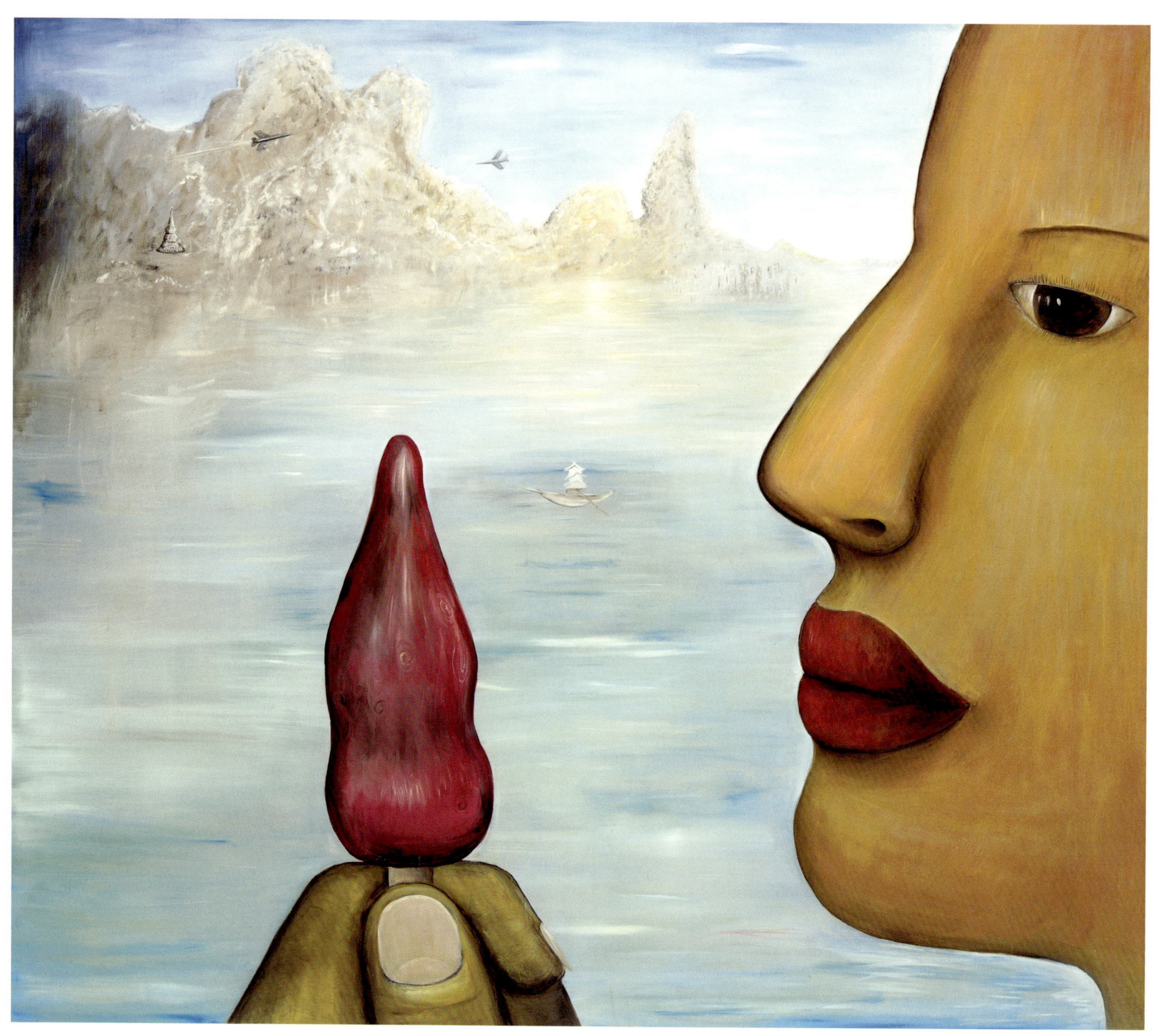

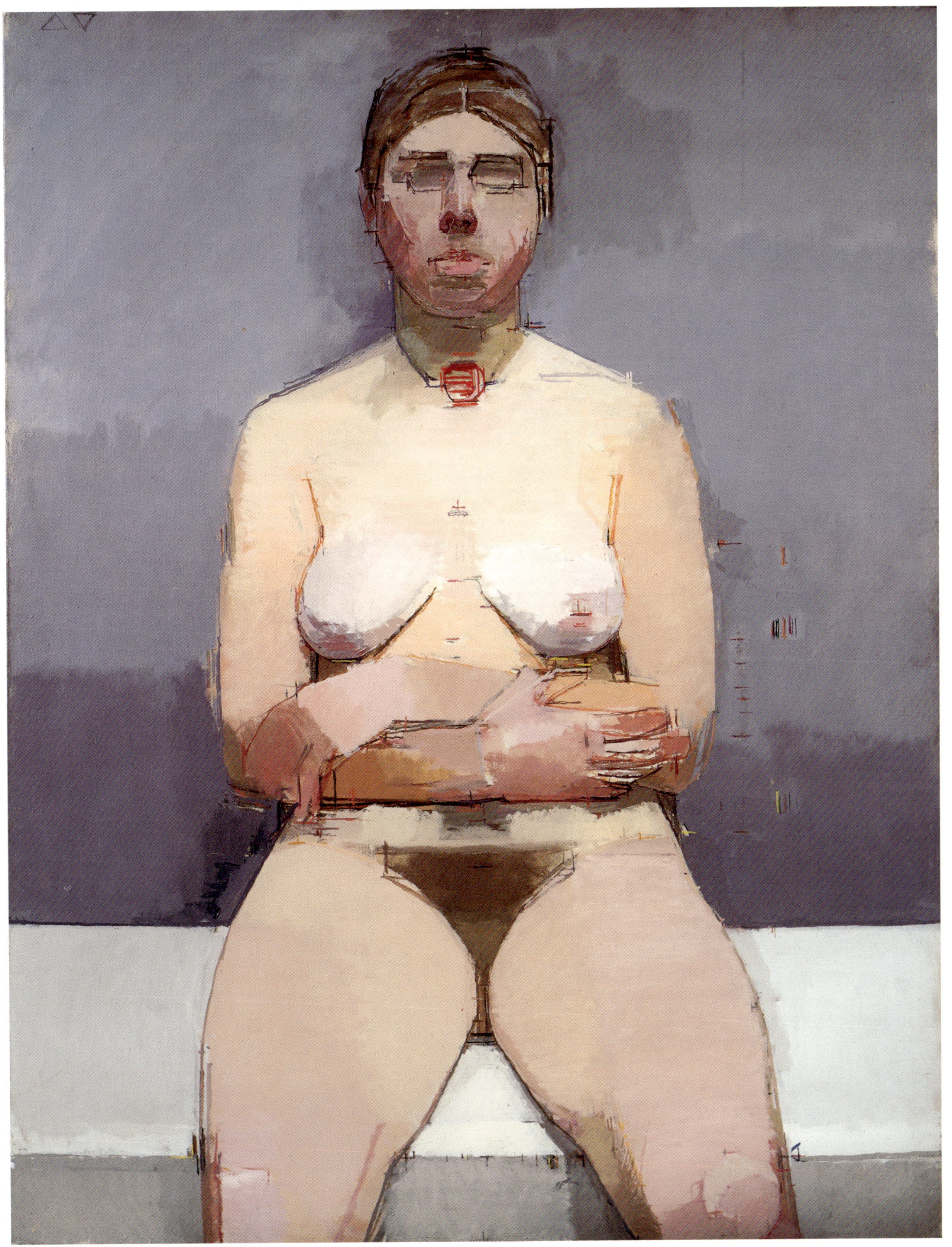

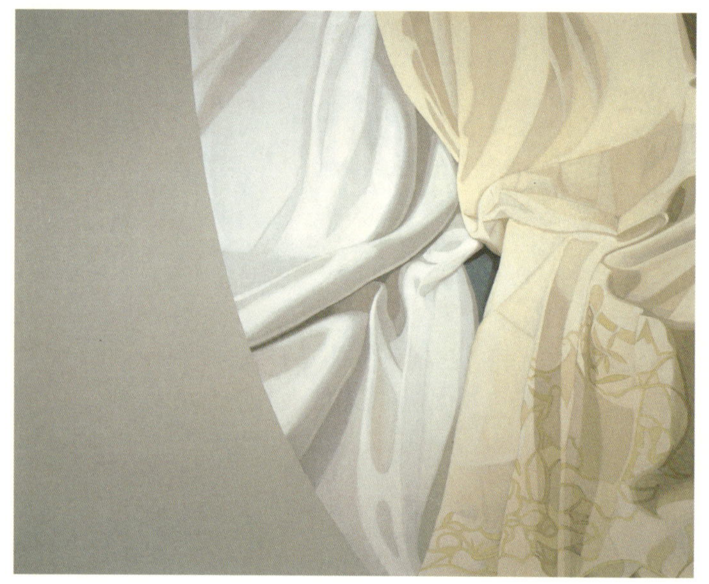

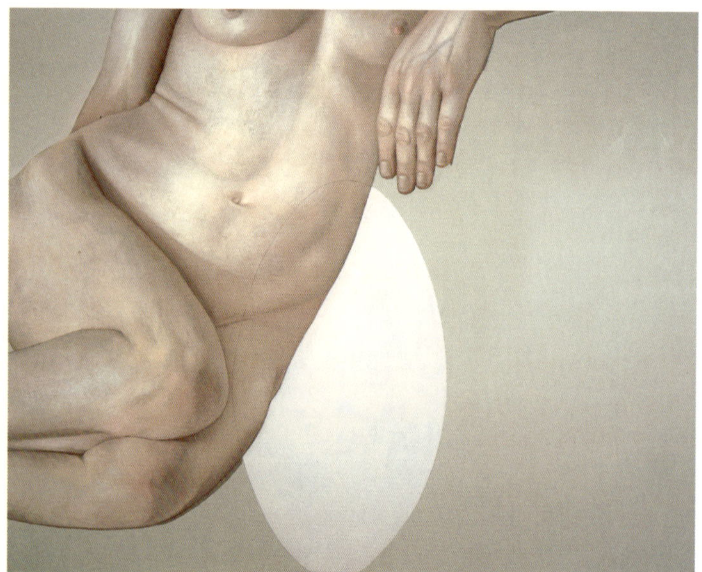

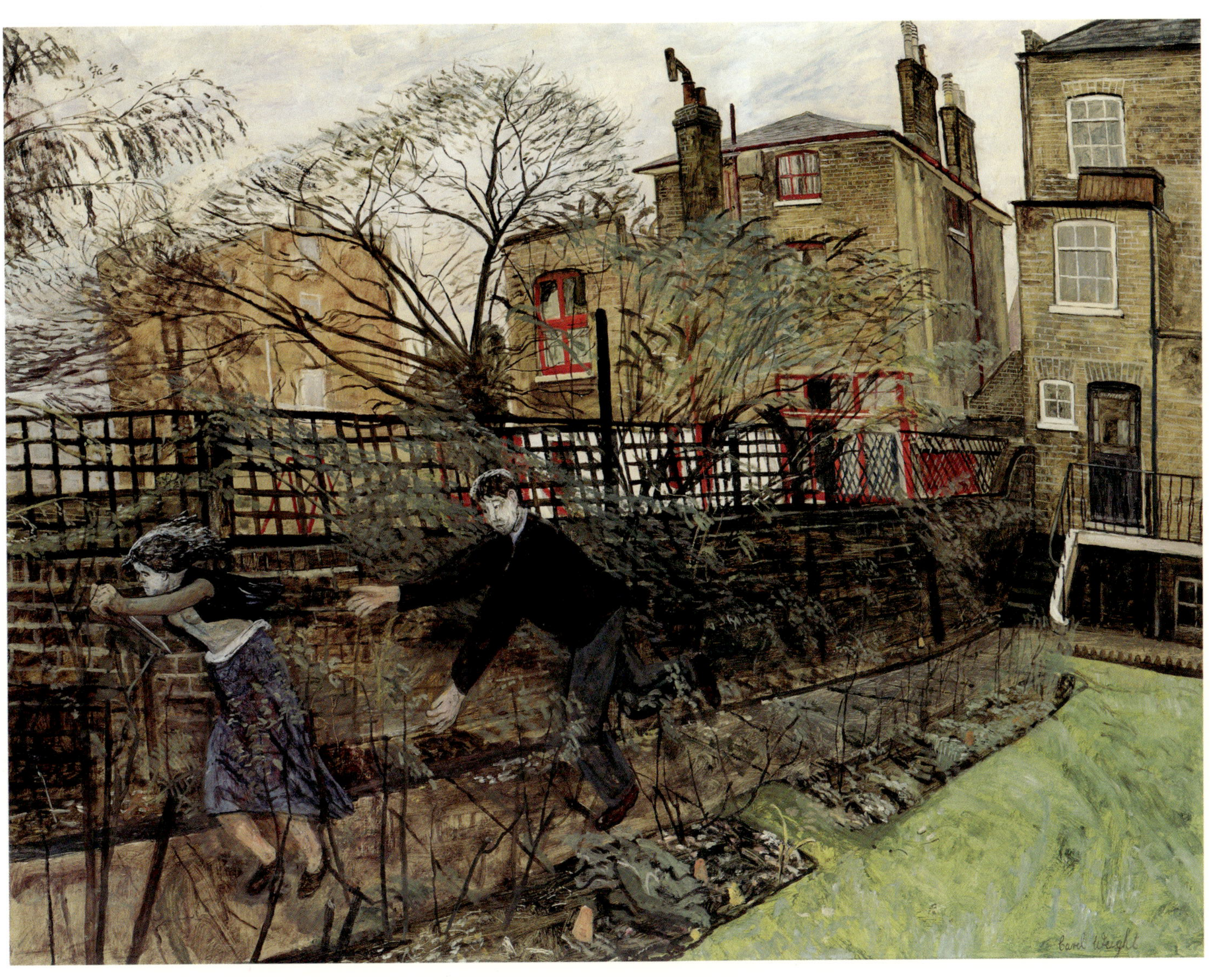
Carel Weight

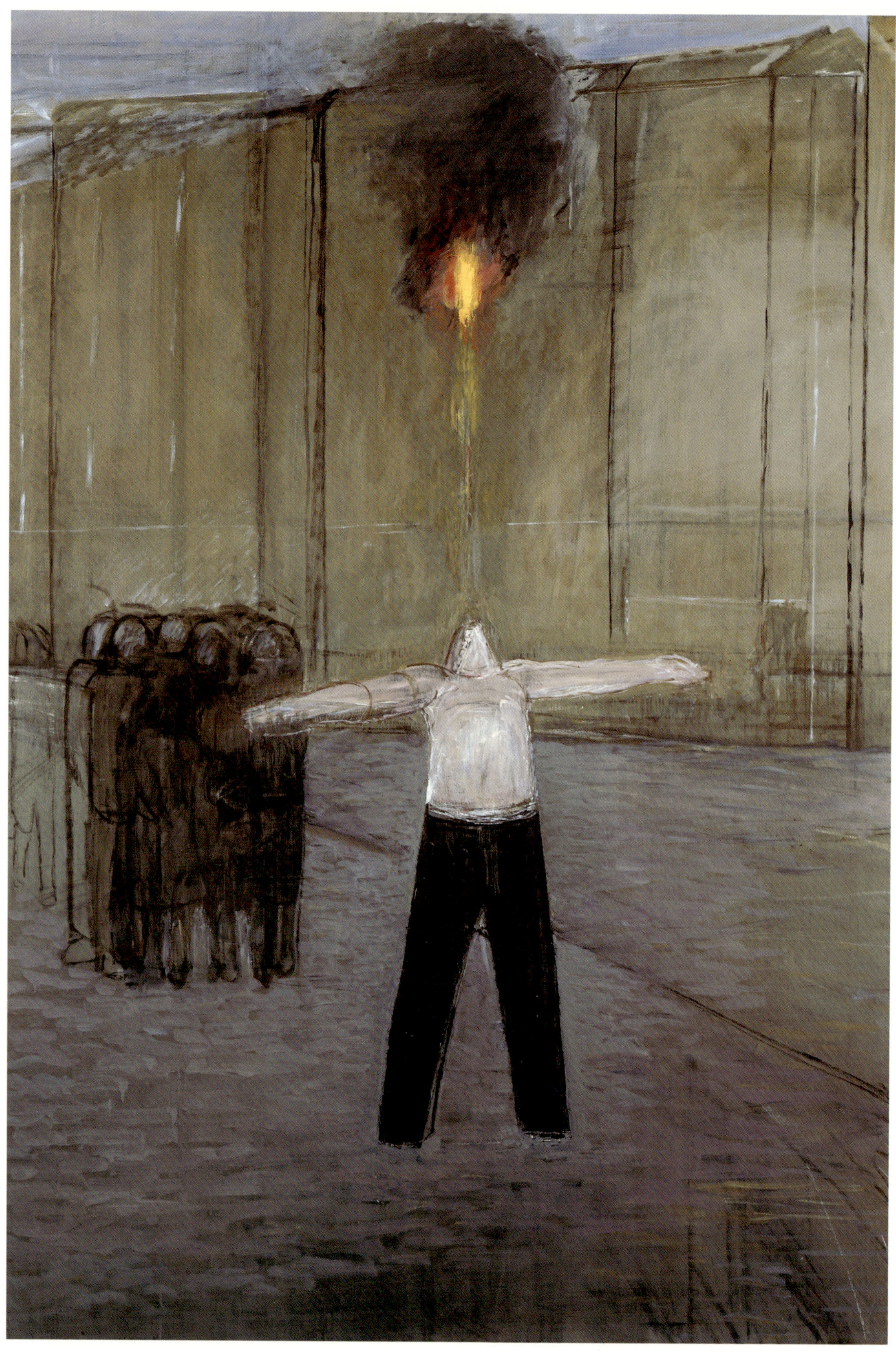

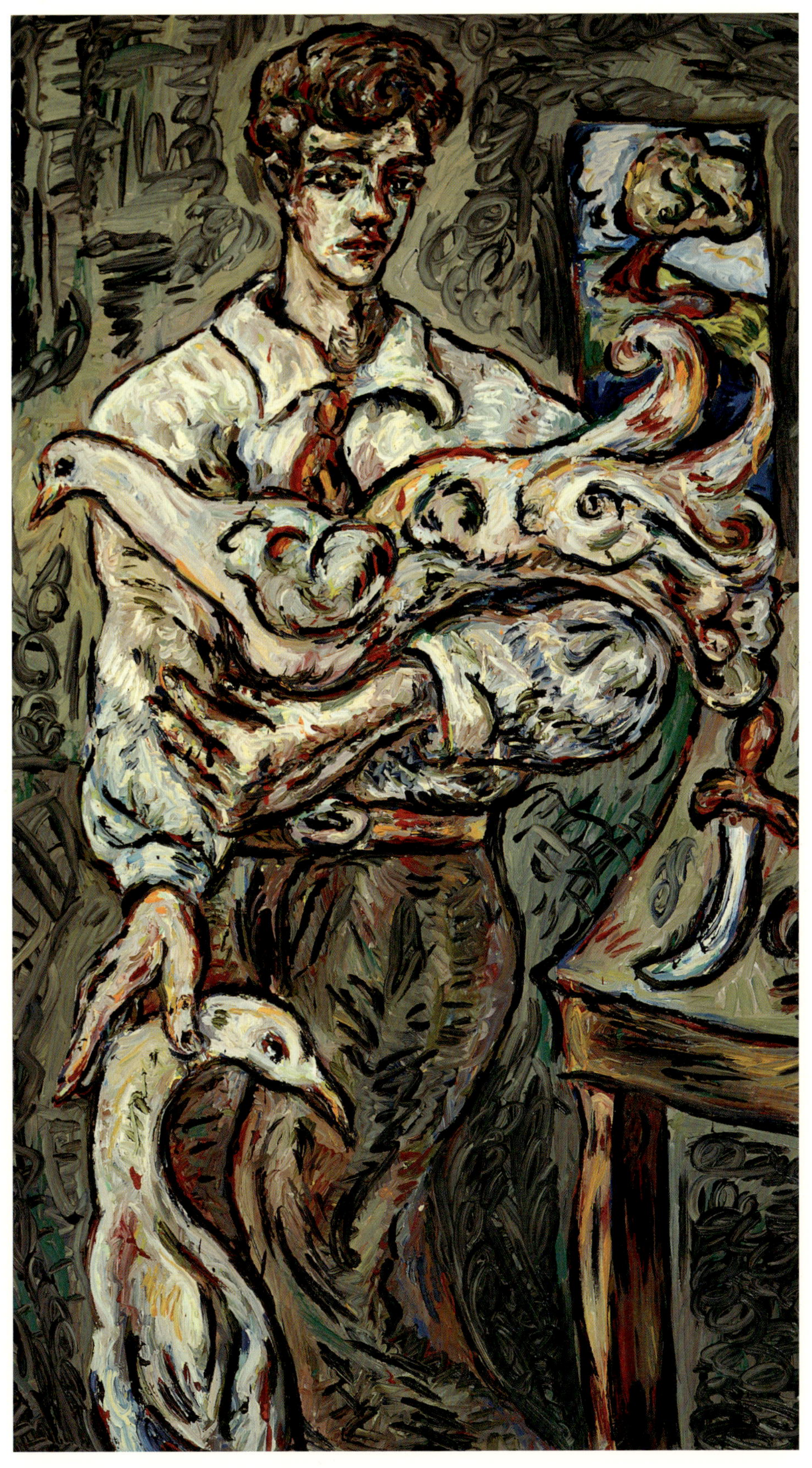

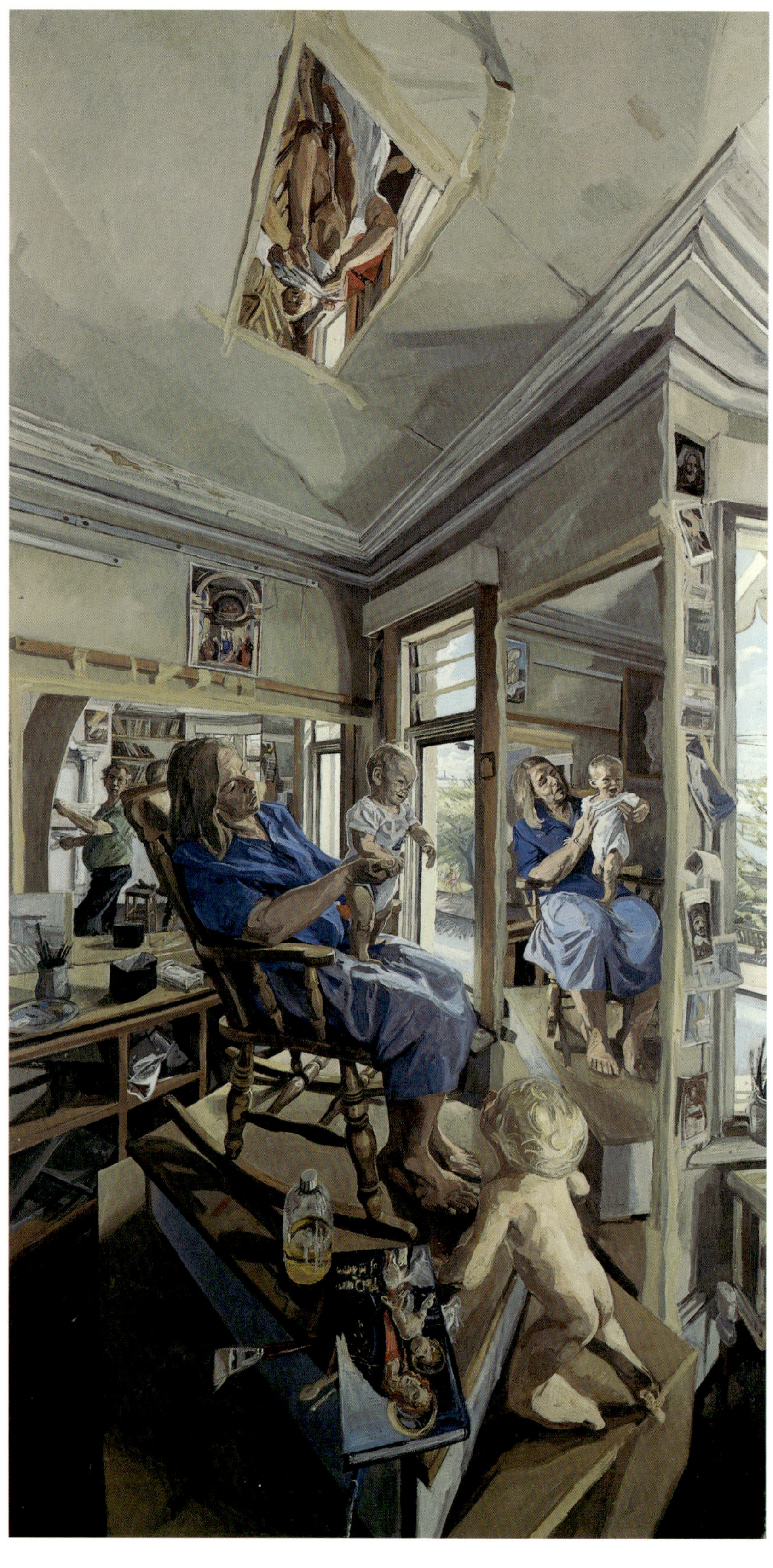

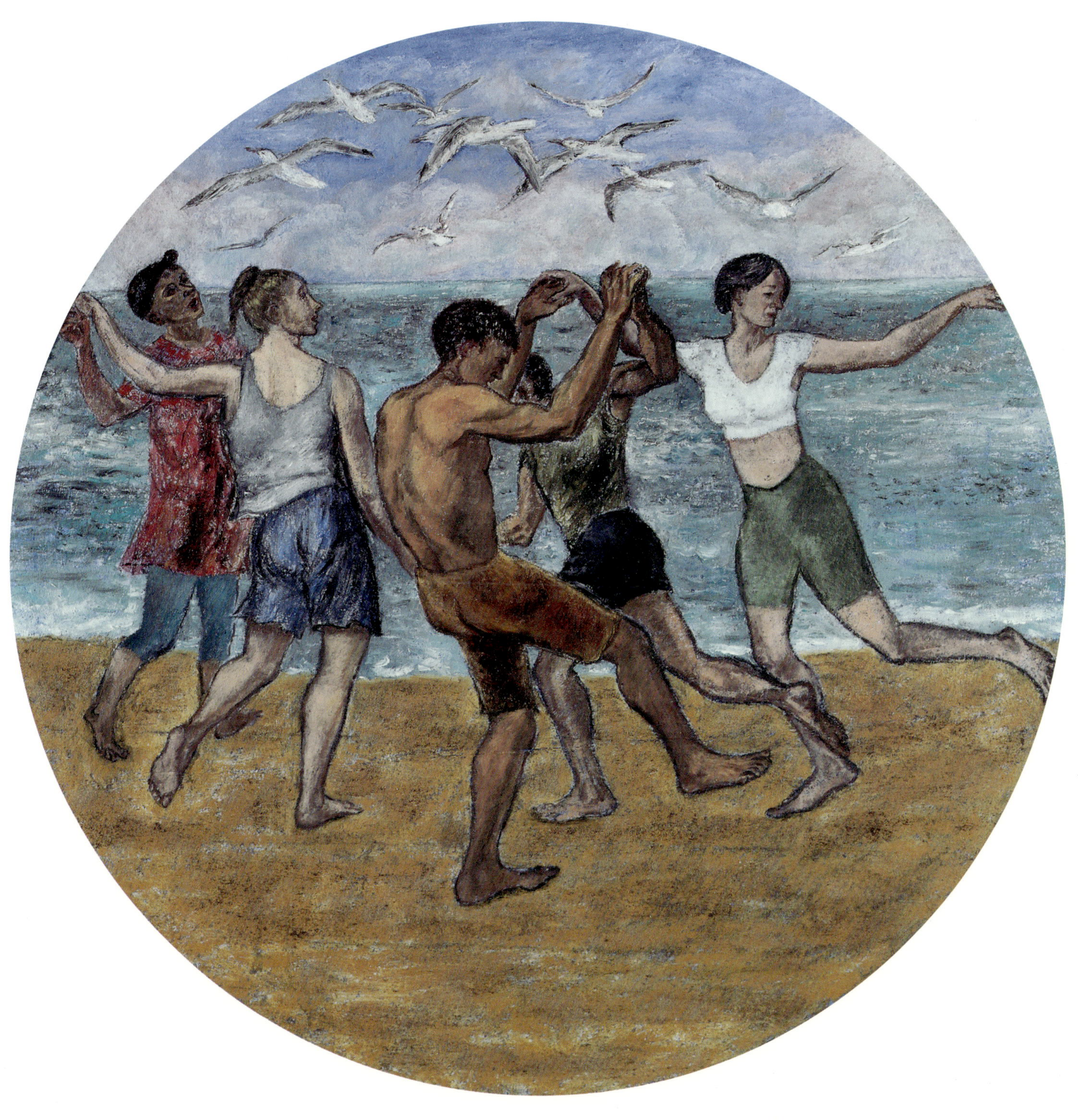

Catalogue

CRAIGIE AITCHISON
Crucifixion 1997
Oil on canvas
24 x 18 cms

FRANK AUERBACH
Gerda Boehm (leaning on her hand) 1980
Oil on canvas
45.7 x 55.9 cms
Courtesy: Marlborough Gallery

JOHN BELLANY
Vesperland 1996
Oil on canvas
203 x 177.5 cms

TONY BEVAN
The Room, Man with Arm Extended 1985
Oil on canvas
167.5 x 167.5 cms
Private Collection

PETER BLAKE
Portraits of Dwarfs after Velasquez IV 1996
Oil on canvas
30.5 x 25.6 cms
Courtesy: Waddington Galleries

DEREK BOSHIER
Viewfinder 1996
Oil on canvas
91 x 122 cms
Courtesy: Connaught Brown

BOYD & EVANS
Toll Bridge 1991
Oil on canvas
76 x 457.5 cms

JEFFERY CAMP
Rain, Bored, Thames 1989-90
Oil on canvas
305 x 152.5 cms
Courtesy: Browse & Darby

STEVEN CAMPBELL
The Branch Secretaries 1990
Oil on canvas
182.9 x 170.2 cms
Courtesy: Marlborough Gallery

STEPHEN CHAMBERS
Twins (in Rain) 1997
Oil on canvas
188 x 243 cms

STEPHEN CONROY
Something Special for Tea 1988
Oil on canvas
123 x 101 cms
Collection of Susan Kasen Summer and Robert D. Summer

EILEEN COOPER
Rivers in the Sky 1996
Oil on canvas
153 x 213 cms
Courtesy: Jason & Rhodes

KEN CURRIE
Three Studies of the Human Head I 1996
Oil on canvas
38 x 38 cms
Courtesy: Boukamel Contemporary Art

SIMON EDMONDSON
Sequence 1996
Oil on canvas
149 x 125 cms

LUCIAN FREUD
Benefits Supervisor Sleeping 1995
Oil on canvas
150 x 219 cms
Private Collection, London

PAUL GOPAL CHOWDHURY
On and On 1996
Oil on canvas
144 x 162 cms

ANTHONY GREEN
Anxiety – The Two Bedrooms at Embassy Lodge 1991-4
Oil on canvas
233 x 247 cms
Courtesy: Piccadilly Gallery

MAGGI HAMBLING
Clapham, 85
Oil on canvas
61 x 61 cms
Courtesy: Marlborough Gallery

JOSEF HERMAN
Mother and Child 1993-97
Oil on canvas
122 x 91.5 cms

DAVID HOCKNEY
Left: Maurice Payne, December 10 1996
Oil on canvas
35 x 27.4 cms

Right: Richard Schmidt, December 12 1996
Oil on canvas
35 x 27.4 cms

PETER HOWSON
Io 1997
Oil on canvas
240 x 180 cms

TIMOTHY HYMAN
Mid River (The Bearer) 1994-97
Oil on canvas
152.5 x 122 cms

BILL JACKLIN
Unloading the Truck 36th Street 1997
Oil on canvas
137.2 x 152.4 cms
Courtesy: Marlborough Gallery

ANDRZEJ JACKOWSKI
The Laboratory Assistant 1994
Oil on canvas
152.4 x 162.5 cms
Courtesy: Purdy Hicks

ALLEN JONES
The Visitor 1984
Oil on canvas
244 x 234 cms

LUCY JONES
Going Swimming 1997
Oil on canvas
218 x 156.5 cms

JOHN KEANE
Struggle with Truth 1996
Oil and mixed media on canvas
209 x 163 cms

KEN KIFF
Man & Woman 1975-90
Oil on canvas
134.6 x 122 cms
Courtesy: Marlborough Gallery

JOHN KIRBY
A Good Child 1997
Oil on canvas
122.5 x 62 cms

R.B. KITAJ
Bad Teeth 1996
Oil on canvas
62 x 51 cms
Courtesy: Marlborough Gallery

HENRY KONDRACKI
Fun Fair 1997
Oil on canvas
183 x 152.5 cms

LEON KOSSOFF
Portrait of Chaim No 2 1997
Oil on canvas
102.2 x 76.2 cms
Private Collection, London

ANSEL KRUT
Venus and Adonis 1996
Oil on canvas
188 x 165 cms
Courtesy: Jason & Rhodes

JOHN LESSORE
Collioure; Chateau Royal,
green bikini 1996/7
Oil on canvas
127.6 x 162 cms
Courtesy: Theo Waddington Fine Art

LEONARD McCOMB
Portrait of Sylvia Passella 1981
Watercolour on paper mounted
on cotton
242.5 x 194 cms
Collection of the Artist

JOCK McFADYEN
Brandenburg 1991
Oil on canvas
203.5 x 115 cms

ISHBEL MYERSCOUGH
Head 1997
Oil on board
91.5 x 61 cms
Courtesy: Anthony Mould Ltd

VICTOR NEWSOME
Model Seeking Tobacco 1997
Egg tempera
105.2 x 114.5 cms
Courtesy: Grosvenor Gallery

HUMPHREY OCEAN
Portrait of Janice Tchalenko 1993
Oil on canvas
59.5 x 49.5 cms

CELIA PAUL
Diptych 1996
Oil on canvas
152.4 x 122 cms (each panel)
Courtesy: Marlborough Gallery

TOM PHILLIPS
The Great Bar 1991
Oil on canvas
33.5 x 43.5 cms

PATRICK PROCKTOR
Ghurka 1983
Oil on canvas
76 x 50.5 cms
Courtesy: Redfern Gallery

PAULA REGO
The Cadet and his Sister 1988
Oil on canvas
213.5 x 152.5 cms
Collection of Susan Kasen Summer and
Robert D. Summer

RAY RICHARDSON
Places and Spaces 1997
Oil on canvas
274 x 152.5 cms
Courtesy: Beaux Arts

MICK ROONEY
Last Supper 1996
Tempera
52.7 x 78 cms
Courtesy: Mercury Gallery

JENNY SAVILLE
Untitled 1994
Oil on canvas
284.5 x 167.6 cms
Collection of Susan Kasen Summer and
Robert D. Summer

TAI-SHAN SCHIERENBERG
Head (James Reed) 1997
Oil on canvas
137 x 121.5 cms

EMMA SERGEANT
Ninib 1996
Oil on gessoed panel
61 x 46 cms

KEVIN SINNOTT
Fallen Man V 1993
Oil on canvas
247 x 173 cms

ANDREW STAHL
Lollipop 1996
Oil on canvas
200 x 225 cms

EUAN UGLOW
Nude with Red Necklace 1970
Oil on canvas
101.5 x 76.2 cms
Courtesy: Browse & Darby

ALISON WATT
Left: Mme Rivière 1997
Oil on canvas
152.4 x 182.9 cms

Right: Fragment V 1997
Oil on canvas
152.4 x 182.9 cms

CAREL WEIGHT
Death of Lucretia 1963
Oil on canvas
101.5 x 127 cms
Private Collection, Crane Kalman Ltd

KARL WESCHKE
The Fire Eater
(With Spectators) 1984-6
Oil on canvas
183 x 122 cms

ADRIAN WISZNIEWSKI
Man with a Brace 1989
Oil on canvas
213 x 122 cms
Collection of Susan Kasen Summer and
Robert D. Summer

JOHN WONNACOTT
Mother & Child with Ceiling,
Mirror, Putti 1994
Oil on canvas
240 x 180 cms
Courtesy: Agnew's

LAETITIA YHAP
Dance to the Music of Time 1996
Oil on board
98 cms (diam)